REFUGE IN THE BLACK DECK

Caitlin Press Inc., 8100 Alderwood Road,
Halfmoon Bay, BC V0N 1Y1
www.caitlin-press.com

Cover by Vici Johnstone
Text design by Vici Johnstone and Tellwell Talent
Edited by Betsy Nuse and Betsy Warland
Front cover photo Ben Dunfield
Printed in Canada

Caitlin Press Inc. acknowledges financial support from the
Government of Canada and the Canada Council for the Arts, and
the Province of British Columbia through the British Columbia
Arts Council and the Book Publisher's Tax Credit.

Library and Archives Canada Cataloguing in Publication
Peffers, Nicola
[Black deck]
        Refuge in the black deck : the story of ordinary seaman
Nicola Peffers / Nicola Peffers.
Originally published under title: Black deck.
ISBN 978-1-987915-43-3 (softcover)
        1. Peffers, Nicola. 2. Sexual harassment in the military—Canada.
3. Women sailors—Canada—Biography. 4. Women sailors—Crimes
against—Canada. 5. Canada—Armed Forces Women. 6. Post-traumatic stress
disorder—Patients—Canada Biography. 7. Peffers, Nicola—Health.
I. Title. II. Title: Black deck.

UB785.C3P44 2017   355.1'334   C2017-900077-2

REFUGE IN THE
BLACK DECK

THE STORY OF
ORDINARY SEAMAN
NICOLA PEFFERS

NICOLA PEFFERS

CAITLIN PRESS

Some of the names in this book have been changed to protect the privacy of the individuals.

*I dedicate this book to all the women and men who have
suffered mental, physical and sexual abuse while
serving their country.
Please know that you are not alone.*

Table of Contents

Meeting the Boat   1
Meeting the Shop   4
Girl (Youngest OD Afloat)   9
Motion   15
My First Bong-Bongs   21
Weather Decks   26
Weather Witch   30
CBRN Training   32
Who Will You Fuck in a Foreign Port?   36
Okinawa   41
Two Beers Per Person Per Day Perhaps   48
Know Your Shit   51
Know Your Ship   53
Busan   62
My First Watch   65
The Watches   71
Drills   79
A New Weapon   88
Crossing the Line   91
Super-All-Nighters   95
Winnipeg Prepares to Fight   97
Action   101
ET Phone Home   104
Tension on the Line   107
Warning Shots   110
Figuring It Out   114
Natural Beauty   122
Cold Showers   124
Bad News Ice Cream   126
Feeling the Motors   128
Cesspool   132

Fucked   135
Day Fifty-Seven   141
Accused   146
The Trial   150
I'm Cute   156
Should'a Fucked Him   158
Birds   160
The EO Wants to Talk to Me   163
Fresh Water Pump #2   167
Ugly Like Me   170
Halfway There   172
Load Shedding   176
The Coxn's Punishment   179
How To Use a Socket Set   183
Gash   188
Padre   191
Tonga   194
Infamous   196
Gate Sentry   202
The Black Deck   206
Channel Fever   209
Life After Deployment   211
Worthless   217
Flashbacks   219
I Can Never Go Back   220
Fugue   223
How I Remember Her   225
Finding a Place   226
Glossary of Navy Speak   228
Acknowledgements   232

MEETING THE BOAT

Walking along a dock in Pearl Harbor, I see her for the first time. I know it's her because of the bright red and white Canadian flag flying from the mast. She doesn't fit in with the rest of the US Navy's grey battle-ships. Her hull is a greyish-green colour unique to the Canadian Navy. I heard in one of my classes that this colour provides better camouflage in fog banks close to the horizon.

Her name is HMCS *Winnipeg*, and I'm her newest crew member. My name is Ordinary Seaman Nicola Peffers, service number november-four-three-seven-zero-four-nine-zero-nine, Marine Electrician. It's 2009, I'm twenty-six years old, and I'm about as green and excited as they come. I joined the military because I wanted to serve my country. The Navy promised the most travel, and I wanted to see the world. Joining the Navy also guaranteed that I'd live on the west coast of Canada. Lush old-growth forests I glimpsed as a child on vacation away from Alberta drew me like a moth to a flame. I picked my trade, marine electrician, because it's a hard sea trade, meaning my entire career would be car-ried out on ship. Sparing myself service in Afghanistan, instead I would conduct peacekeeping roles which the Navy solely does while Canada herself is not threatened by war.

My last training class ended Friday. Today is Sunday. I sail with the ship into a six-month NATO deployment first thing tomorrow morning. Today will be my first day on a ship. Ever. After Basic Training, trade training, and a quick seamanship course I'm definitely ready for this. I hear there's a medal for us at the end! I will be the first in my Basic

Training platoon to be deployed and the first to get a medal. I couldn't have asked for a better opportunity to advance my new career.

I pause, seeing a perfect photo opportunity. A few of the people travelling in my group stop with me. We're mostly newly posted crew members, but the rest of them are senior Non-Commissioned Officers (NCO).

I whip out my camera and catch a beautiful shot of the bow of the ship and part of her port side with the afternoon sun in the background. The sunlight makes the red parts of the flag glow brightly, and a swell of patriotic pride rises in me. Then I hear a voice near us.

"Excuse me, ma'am, excuse me!" Turning around, I see a uniformed member of the US Military Police jogging over to my location. We turn to greet him. "No photography, there's a sign right over there." He points, and I see that he's right. No more than three metres away, at the edge of the dock, is a sign saying No Photography.

The MP asks us all for ID, and we dig in our pockets to produce our military ID cards. Once he inspects them and gives them back to us, he turns to me again.

"I need to see your camera." He holds out his hand. I hesitate. Not my camera! I don't want to lose all the pictures I've taken. He sees my hesitation. "I need to delete the picture you just took," he tells me.

I grudgingly hand over my camera and watch while he thumbs through some buttons to delete the picture. He hands the camera back to me.

"I'm gonna need your name, unit, and a contact in your chain of command," he says in a serious tone of voice while he prepares to write in a notepad.

I cringe. I haven't even stepped onto the boat yet, and I'm in trouble. How could I have missed that sign?

"Um, my name is Ord..." I start to talk, but one of the senior NCOs interrupts me and steps forward.

"I'm Chief Tallow, and we're all heading to the *Winnipeg* over there," he motions toward the small greenish ship. "This is OS Peffers' first time on an American base. I think this is just a basic misunderstanding. I'll personally make sure her chain of command is informed of her behaviour."

I get a sinking feeling in the pit of my stomach and start awkwardly inspecting my shoes. Having just gotten off the plane, we're all dressed in civilian clothing. Canadian Forces personnel don't travel in uniform for international safety reasons.

The MP cocks his head to one side and makes a show of thinking it over. Then he closes and puts away his notepad.

"Make sure she reads the signs in the future," he tells the chief, then he bids us a good afternoon and walks away.

We start walking toward the boat again and CPO 2 Tallow tells me that it's always best to be the first to tell your chain of command if you screw up; that way they hear it from you first and it makes you look responsible. Following sheepishly, I gaze up at the *Winnipeg* as we approach. The last thing I want to do is get in trouble.

MEETING THE SHOP

Following a line of people heading down a hatch in the fo'c'sle, I'm amazed at how nimbly people walk down the steep ladder. They grasp at the deckhead for handholds as they go. I teeter awkwardly on the rungs, turning to hug the ladder like we were shown in a safety video. This promptly causes a traffic jam as it drastically slows my progress down the ladder. To make matters worse, I'm lugging a huge hockey bag with all my kit for the next half a year. A few male Leading Seamen offer to help me with my bag, and between the two of them they have it taken down to two deck.

My helpers welcome me to the ship and tell me to find a rack and locker in a female Mess. One Mess just happens to be right next to the series of ladders I just climbed down. Thanking them, I open the door to the Mess.

The second-last available female rack is a top rack; the two racks below are already taken. It's to my immediate right, bolted to the false bulkhead which creates a thin wall within the confines of a real bulkhead. I dump my bag on the deck, find the ship's office, and spend the rest of the afternoon doing as much of my In Routine as possible.

In Routine is a ritual that every newly posted member must perform. A file is hand-carried to all corners of the base or ship to get signatures for things like the Mess and the post office; this proves that you have arrived. Most people consider it to be a boring chore. I don't mind it; I'm getting paid to walk around and meet new people.

Once I find the ship's laundry room, I make up my rack. There are no free lockers left in one Mess since it holds a bunch of compressed-air bottles for firefighting. A locker is found for me in seven Mess just below one Mess and right next to the female Heads. There are lots of wandering around, lost moments. People are nice about giving me directions though.

Winnipeg is so much bigger on the inside! I'm in a giant metal maze. Tiny corridors called flats branch off everywhere and connect to ladders. And there's a flow to traffic. There are arrow stickers next to each ladder indicating if it's an up or a down ladder. Everything is cramped, compact, close together. Wherever a few metres of spare deck space can be found, a treadmill or a stationary bike has been bolted to the deck. Things are packed in densely along the bulkheads. Firefighting equipment, emergency breathing apparatus, pipes, and cables are everywhere.

I meet two corporals in one Mess and introduce myself.

"Hi, I'm OS Peffers," I shake hands with them both.

"I'm Cpl Kenneth, the baby doc on-board," one says. Baby doc is slang for the junior physician's assistant.

"And I'm Cpl Biscoe, one of the clerks."

Kenneth and Biscoe go back to talking among themselves for a minute or so, and I try to think of something to say.

"So, have you guys been off base yet?" I finally ask a little shyly.

"We were just leaving to go to the mall, it's just a few minutes' walk from the gate," Biscoe says.

There's a pregnant pause, then Kenneth says, "Like to join us?" I get the impression they're just being polite, but I'd like to go ashore.

"Sure, thanks." I smile awkwardly.

At the mall's food court we order food and find a table. Kenneth and Biscoe order Chinese food, and I order a fruit smoothie. We eat in silence. Feeling awkward, I ask questions to fill the silence.

"So, how long have you guys been posted to the *Winnipeg*?"

Kenneth replies, "About a year and a half."

Biscoe adds, "Just over two years."

More silence. I slurp my smoothie for a few more long minutes and ask another question.

"How do you guys like it on *Winnipeg*?"

Biscoe shrugs, "S'okay."

Kenneth swallows her mouthful of food and says, "It's fine."

Neither of them look up from their food. Again more silence. I slurp more smoothie. There's an aloofness to the way they just sit and eat. They don't seem the least bit interested in me, and the awkwardness grows. I wonder if they don't like me. Really wanting to be liked, I spend the rest of the time in silence, feeling out of place.

That evening the duty driver takes me to Dukes, the Honolulu bar that everyone goes to. I've been told to meet up with the people of my shop there. The bar is crowded, and I make my way between the tables to the outside patio. I recognize PO 1 Greg Robertson from the few brief meetings we had back at the Fleet School. It was an insane ten days' notice to deploy while I finished up my trade exams and carried out all the appointments and the mound of paperwork necessary to deploy. Normally people are supposed to receive months of notice before deploying, but that doesn't always happen.

PO 1 Robertson is the head of my department. He's wearing a Hawaiian shirt and talking animatedly to a group at the table. The table is bulging with drinks and empty glasses. He sees me and stands up, spreading his arms.

"Peffers!" he yells while he grins at me. The rest of the table turns to look.

"Hi, PO," I say, smiling politely.

He pulls up a chair for me. He explains that I'm the newest addition to the shop, then he goes around the table, one person at a time, introducing me to my new co-workers. The other ordinary seamen are Dale, Kelvin, JD, and Holloway; they look quite drunk. I waste no time ordering myself a drink to join them. The leading seamen are Stafford, Alders, and Pellier. Stafford looks the drunkest at the table. Alders, who is sitting next to me, leans toward me and tells me she'll be my supervisor. Alders is the only other female in my department. Last but not least, there are PO 2 Perrant, PO 2 Mann (who tells me he's my new training PO), and PO 2 Hampton. Basically, as an ordinary seaman, anyone with a higher rank than me is considered my boss.

After the introductions, the people go back to their conversations. Robertson leans his elbows on the table and rests his chin in his hands, sitting right across from me. He stares at me intently from behind his drink with a scheming sort of smile on his face, studying me. Sizing me up. I look him in the eyes and smile politely. He just keeps looking me directly in the eyes. I hold his gaze for longer than I think is socially acceptable, starting to shake my head, shrug my shoulders.

"What?"

He continues to stare with a knowing kind of expression.

"What?" I ask again, continuing to return his stare.

This strange exchange continues for a few more seconds. I refuse to look away. Finally, he breaks the eye contact to take a sip of his drink and the moment is over. Alders starts to talk to me.

"The PO 1 tells me you like to work out."

"I do!" I smile and lean in close to hear her over the noise at the table, glancing at her muscular arms. "I see you do too."

Alders smiles, "Yeah, it's my thing, working out."

"Totally." I smile and sip my drink.

"You've got some muscle on you as well," she observes. We're both wearing tank tops.

"Thanks, I worked hard for it!"

"I have a feeling we'll get along just fine," Alders says. She has a beautiful smile.

Getting along fine reminds me then of getting in trouble and what that chief said to me back on the dock. Alders is my supervisor after all.

"I have something to tell you," I say, apprehension dawning.

Alders meets my gaze with glacier-blue eyes.

"I took a photograph of the *Winnipeg*, and one of the American MPs caught me. I was with a few chiefs and they said my chain of command would be informed..." I trail off nervously, then ask, "Am I in trouble?"

Alders laughs. "No, I don't think so, but I'll let the PO 1 know about it. Thanks for telling me."

I smile then, relaxing somewhat. I spend a good Navy evening getting drunk with my new department. Robertson takes the time to explain that we are a tight shop and everyone gets along. Any problems that arise are dealt with from within the department. He says any one of them would be willing to help me out as I get my sea legs. Stories are passed around, and lots of laughs are had. I'm told that I'm the new molly for the first leg of the voyage. The other ODs cheer at it not being one of them. Molly is the Navy term for the dishwashers on-board. I shrug good-naturedly at my job description. I'm just happy to be part of the sail. Everyone is excited about a rumoured anti-piracy mission. These are my people.

GIRL (YOUNGEST OD AFLOAT)

Waking up to a pipe and "wakey-wakey hands to breakfast," excitement hits me again. Today we sail out of Hawaii. I make up my rack and head down the ladder a little less awkwardly now. After changing into my uniform and going to the Heads, I emerge. The ship is full of people milling about, and everyone in the flats turns sideways to step past other people. There's usually a nod or a brief "Hi."

So far I know how to get to my rack, locker, and Heads. The rest of the ship is a maze. Alders finds me outside the Heads, and I'm relieved to see a familiar face.

"There you are," she says, smiling warmly.

"Oh, I'm glad to see you," I smile back.

"Come on, this way to breakfast," Alders motions with her arm for me to follow her and she starts walking down the flats. She shows me the way to the junior ranks' Mess. It's only a short walk. "This is where all our meals are taken."

"Okay."

There's a short line forming at the steam table where people stand with plastic trays and metal utensils. We get in line. Rock music wafts out from the galley, and everyone seems to be smiling and in good spirits. There's plenty of hot food for breakfast: eggs, sausages, bacon, and oatmeal. Once I fill my tray I follow Alders through a doorway into the Mess.

Emerging into one of the largest compartments on ship, completely crowded with people, Alders turns to me.

"It's referred to as the Cave."

Along the aft wall is a counter with toasters, coffee pots, juice dispensers, and a fridge. Five long tables with benches on the right line the starboard bulkhead. There's a counter running along the centre line of the ship.

Behind the counter on the left or port side of the compartment are a dozen plush-looking black leather love seats and a large flat-screen TV mounted on the bulkhead. The long tables are crammed with people eating and talking loudly. Following Alders through the crowd to the second long table close to the forward bulkhead, I take a seat.

"This is our table, we share it with the hull techs."

The table next to ours, closest to the forward bulkhead, belongs to the stokers. It seems to be the liveliest table in the Cave.

It's a tight squeeze onto the bench at our table. Holloway, JD, Kelvin, and Dale are already half-finished eating. Stafford joins us with a bowl of oatmeal and pours hot sauce over it, much to our disgust. Stafford just laughs as he stirs it in.

After breakfast I follow everyone to the shop, where repairs are carried out. The stokers are just aft of our shop.

Our ET shop is very small. It's about the size of a walk-in closet. Twelve people cram in like sardines for the morning meeting. When the ship was being designed, this space was originally supposed to be Medical Stores, but they realized the boat didn't have an ET shop so this space was converted at the last minute. Two counters run along opposite bulkheads lined with technical manuals, tool kits, and a laptop computer. A vice is bolted to one of the counters. Below the counters are a bunch of drawers, some with names on them. I'm given my own drawer full of hand tools.

There's a fair bit of decorative humour in the space. A large Warning Live Power sign is zap strapped to a pipe on the port side. A hazard sign of a person getting electrocuted is displayed on the door.

JD sits at the computer playing Michael Jackson's "Beat It." There are four small speakers zap strapped to the deckhead in each corner of the room. The sound quality is good. People chat and laugh.

"Hey, check this out, Peff," OS Kelvin opens the power panel in the space. The inside is covered with colourful pictures of smiling, silly people. "It's called the Party Panel."

"Oh?" I take a moment to glance at the photographs and smile before Kelvin closes it up again.

I glance around and notice all the faces from the previous evening. PO 1 Robertson, the most senior ET on-board, starts to talk. Duties are assigned and the other ODs are told where they are on the watch rotation. PO 1 Robertson tells me to report to PO 1 Davin in the galley once I finish my In Routine at the coxn's office.

PO 2 Mann, who looks a little worse for wear from last night, hands me three booklets he refers to as training packages, my work for the next six months. It's a coincidence that the sail is six months and the first six months on-board ship is the phase of being double-banked (where you complete your training packages). All my training will take place on a deployment. This is highly irregular. Most new members are alongside but not deployed for their first six months, or just do short sails.

Glancing briefly through the books, I see the small one is called *Know Your Ship*. It's full of empty drawings of the various decks and sections of a Canadian Patrol Frigate. I'm to fill in by hand all the details of the various systems such as fire mains. Next is a yellow Duo-Tang full of tables listing all the electrical systems on-board and spaces for signatures and dates. I have to learn each system and be able to explain how they work to a PO 2 or higher as well as draw out the system on an engineering drawing book. If my work and presentation are acceptable, they sign off on that system. Once all are signed off, I have to pass an oral board in front of my chain of command up to the EO (engineering officer). Only then do I earn my watch as an electrician of the watch (ETOW).

"But that's sexual harassment..."

The PO 1 calls the meeting to a close, and I step out into the flats again. After a couple of wrong turns and some friendly advice I find the coxn's office. The coxswain is the highest ranking senior NCO and is in charge of the ship's discipline. If you're ever called to the coxn's office it's usually for some kind of punishment. Busy with paperwork, the coxn barely glances at me as he hands me my ship's ball cap and two ship's crest badges to sew onto my black uniform jackets.

Walking down the flats, I inspect my new bits of uniform. The black ball cap is something I've been waiting for. "FFH 338 HMCS *Winnipeg*" is written across the front in gold embroidery. I find my way back to my locker in seven Mess without getting lost this time, and putting the hat on, I adjust it for size and inspect myself in my locker mirror. My short blond hair is tucked behind my ears. My freckled face is smiling with my blue eyes behind my glasses. My uniform looks good: blue button-up shirt and black pants with a black jacket over the shirt. Now I officially belong to a ship, and I no longer have to wear my Basic Training black beret. I look less like a newbie now, which is highly desirable for someone at my rank.

Taking out a red carabiner that I got in preparation for my ball cap, I loop the back of the cap onto the red metal clamp. The carabiner goes on my left rear belt loop. A small LED flashlight and utility knife on my right hip complete the outfit. Every sailor is required to have a flashlight and knife on them at all times when on ship. Next I inspect the badges with the ship's crest: navy blue background with a brown bison standing in the middle of a golden looped circle. I already know the ship's motto: "One with the strength of many."

Walking back to the Cave, I meet up with a handful of junior ranks who are also mollies. They are busy sweeping and cleaning after breakfast. They pause briefly to introduce themselves. One of them, Leading Seaman Coté, tells me they're about to have a meeting with Davin, the senior cook on-board and the person I'll be reporting to now, when I hear "Girl!"

A man's voice is yelling from the doorway. I start to ask LS Coté what I can do to help but I hear it again, only louder this time.

"Girl!"

I turn to see a fat, greying man with a white cook's uniform staring blankly at me. The rest of the ODs have stopped what they're doing.

"GIRL!" He barks it like a drill command while he makes a show of leaning toward me.

I'm shocked. I've never been addressed like this before. Simply by my gender? I've been called many things in Basic Training but never like this. My mouth falls open. I don't know what to do.

"GIRL!" he yells again. His face is contorted with anger.

"You can't call me that," I hear myself say. Did I really just say that? "You can address me as Ordinary Seaman or Peffers."

A collective gasp arises around me. The cook is staring me down, the air thick with tension.

"I can call you whatever I like!" PO 1 Davin yells. "And your chain of command will hear about your talking back!"

I feel my face flush.

"Here's the work schedule!" He aggressively tapes a piece of paper to the Cave door. "I better not catch any of you lying around while there's work to do! Now clean up the Cave, it looks like a shit pit!"

Davin points at LS Chester and LS Coté. "Get over to the chief's and PO's Mess now, the dishes are piling up and the fat fucks need to be kept happy!" Then he storms off.

Stunned, I look around at the other ODs, some holding bar cloths, some holding brooms. They all look miserable and submissive.

LS Chester sighs heavily. "Another day in paradise." It's a common military expression, especially when you're being ordered to do something unpleasant. The mollies break up to resume their cleaning. The only other woman in the group, OS Finnerty, comes up to me.

"You should be more careful. You can't talk to a PO 1 like that; you'll only get in trouble."

Finnerty sighs heavily.

"The PO 1 gets grumpy whenever we slip." She motions for me to follow her into the tiny scullery adjacent to the Cave. She starts to run the dishwasher. "He can't smoke while we're closed up."

I recognize the terms: slip is leaving the jetty and closed up is when everyone is at their stations. We're closed up for exit of harbour, and all doors and hatches are closed in defence against running aground while in harbour.

Still a little shocked, I don't know what to say.

"There's nothing you can do about it." She starts wiping down the counter.

"We could lodge a complaint. Respect is an integral part of—"

"Then you'll really be in trouble."

Speechlessly, I watch Finnerty. She looks deflated as she shows me how to use the dishwasher and garburator. I stack the hot, clean plates in my arms and carry them across to the galley; my fear that Davin will tell my chain of command runs wild in my mind.

That evening as I'm heading aft on three deck to look for an empty stationary bike, a chief eyes me as I walk past and I hear him say to the guy next to him, "There goes the youngest OD afloat."

I recognize their term too. Youngest OD afloat is a joking expression in the Navy, referring to SCOPA or senior commanding officer presently afloat, whose presence determines rank order in a Colours ceremony.

MOTION

I feel like I'm drunk, my first few days at sea. I laugh at the way I'm stumbling around, carrying precarious piles of clean and breakable plates back to the galley. I haven't dropped any yet. Unable to walk straight, veering into bulkheads, grabbing at pipes and doorways, the motion that I feel is unlike any other. Within a few hours of starting work as molly, the deck starts to rock slowly from port to starboard, up and down, up and to port, down and to starboard. It moves in all kinds of dimensions with a regular rhythm. There are no windows in a warship except for the CO's dining room and the bridge, so motion is the only sensation I have to tell me that we're under way.

The motion changes depending on where you are in the ship. If you're aft, it's a constant gentle motion. If you're forward, it's a more pronounced rising and falling action as the nose of the ship tends to buck slightly. The motion changes with different sea states as well.

Every few hours, this motion is punctuated by a cook yelling "Molly!" for one of us to go down to the fridge flats and get them an item like a box of broccoli or a bag of flour.

Cold, dizzy, and tired I stumble my way down the ladder to the fridge flats to get more fruit for the fruit bowl. A mental haze has settled in my brain. I'm told by one of the mollies that this is low-grade seasickness. Fortunately, it only lasts for the first forty-eight hours. I start to be able to walk normally again, and the mental haze clears up.

As a molly, I work twelve hours a day cleaning in the Cave. When the watch changes to Firsts (8 p.m.) the white lights in the flats get switched over to a dark-red night lighting. This is to help preserve night vision. At first I find the red lighting strange and alien, but it quickly becomes soothing to me and I even start to look forward to it each evening.

After about a week, the different kinds of motion are more familiar. If we're travelling into the wind, we'll hit the waves perpendicularly and have pitching but not much roll. Walking along the flats, I feel myself getting heavier with every step, then feather light as the bow drops through the wave trough. If the wind is hitting us sideways, then we'll be abeam of the waves, and the deck rolls from side to side as the waves hit our flank, making it hard to walk straight. People lean into the rolls to compensate. Groups of people walk down the flats all leaning at odd angles compared to the bulkheads and door frames, but really they are the ones walking upright.

"Sideways rolls are preferred when people are working because that motion tends to cause less seasickness," explains a leading seaman standing next to me in the food line one afternoon.

"The pitching action is best because it causes less seasickness," another leading seaman standing in line for breakfast one morning assures me.

Everyone seems to have different preferences and tolerances for seasickness and wants to share their own seasickness story with me.

"My first time at sea I was so seasick I was constantly puking so hard I burst blood vessels in my eyes!" one OS hull tech tells me while I scarf down a quick meal before resuming my molly duties.

"One time, there was this Army dude," a leading seaman starts to tell me. "He was all big and brawny and he thought the Navy was a bunch of pussies and he told us that to our faces. He really didn't want to be here." Sitting through another rushed meal, I take a bite and continue to listen. "Well, first time we slip the seas are pretty rough, and within a few hours this guy is so sick he can't even walk anymore. He just sort of curls up on the deck shivering and moaning." The LS stops to laugh. "Well, everyone just ignored him. We all just walked over him and showed him no compassion. After about a day of this the doc had to come along and inject his ass with Gravol." The leading seaman laughs again and continues to eat for a bit. "After that, the tough Army guy had a little more respect."

The rolls are worse when I'm trying to sleep because I have the unshakable feeling that I'm going to roll out of my rack. Each rack on-board is fitted with a seat belt not unlike those in a car so that when the rolls are severe enough you can strap yourself into your rack so you don't fall out. So far, I haven't had to use my seat belt. Yet.

Working out every other day in the crammed with equipment compartment called Reserve Space Two, I find it mostly empty of people except one man whom I begin to recognize. We seem to have the same workout schedule. We start chatting, and he introduces himself as Jed. He's WO Jed MacDowel, the weather witch on-board. Weather witch is Navy speak for meteorologist or met tech.

Every morning immediately following wakey-wakey, Jed gets on the shincom and delivers a morning weather report for everyone to hear: "Good morning, *Winnipeg*. Today's weather is sunny at twenty-seven degrees celcius outside so you may wish to come up and enjoy the sun. The wind is coming from the southeast at fifteen knots..."

He then closes with a joke of the day.

A few weeks later, one of the firefighters, Cpl Slater, gets approval from the CO to start his own morning show: "Good morning, *Winnipeg*. This is Dave, comin' atcha from the bridge where all things seniorly are being decided. Today we have with us a very special person, please welcome the XO." This is the executive officer, or second in command of the ship.

There's a long, muffled pause while the air crackles, then a faint "Hello!" can be heard, barely in range of the shincom's microphone.

"Today our wonderful XO is sporting a sexy pair of sunglasses by Ray-Ban and is on sharp lookout for flying fish, aren't you sir?" There's another long pause, then Slater's voice comes back on the air. "Stoic silence, that's all folks...this man is a machine! And over here we have someone who needs no introductions...well maybe he does, who ever actually sees this guy anyway?..." Slater laughs for a moment, then continues. "The one and only Captain of HMCS *Winnipeg*, the wonderful Cdr Pearse!"

Another pause while the radio crackles.

"Our CO has no comment, folks! And with that it's time for some music..."

One day while on the upper decks, Slater is smoking and I'm taking out the gash. He's talking to some friends, and I pause to listen in. He's nice to me and picks a nickname for me: he calls me Questions because I'm always asking questions. His morning show usually involves some music and some jokes at the expense of the higher ranking people on-board. So far he hasn't been shut down yet.

One morning Slater starts to sample a bunch of songs from a lost iPod that he found. He picks the songs he thinks would embarrass the owner the most and tells us that the iPod can be picked up at the coxn's office by the person who is not embarrassed to admit to owning the Backstreet Boys. The iPod is picked up, but we never do find out who owns it.

That evening while working out, Jed tells me, "Slater was being cruel," as he finishes a set of bench presses.

"Yeah," I pick up a pair of dumbbells, performing a dead lift.

He sits up on his bench and grabs his water bottle. "He shouldn't have done that." He takes a swig.

"Yeah." Another dead lift.

"Course, if anyone found my iPod, they wouldn't find the Backstreet Boys on it!" Jed grins.

I laugh, doing another dead lift. Inwardly I'm suddenly insecure. My iPod actually has a Backstreet Boys song on it. Judgment is quick to be thrown around here.

The next day, I'm carrying a huge pile of teetering plates down the flats to the galley after breakfast is over, and PO 1 Robertson suddenly appears with a camera and says "Say cheese!" as he snaps my picture. I smile and continue with my work.

At seven days at sea, it's traditional to get some kind of hazing ceremony. Kelvin, Dale, and JD sneak into my Mess while I'm working in the Cave and completely cover my rack in thick layers of plastic food wrap. OS Chelsea, a steward who sleeps directly below me, laughs when she sees me sawing through thick layers of plastic with my knife so I can go to bed.

When I'm not working, sleeping or working out I'm working on my training packages. My *Know Your Ship* booklet guides me through her deck by deck, section by section. I walk around the flats using it the way a tourist would use a map. After about a week I can get my way around to most locations. I like it, the act of moving through my ship, going up the ladders, opening hatches, dogging doors closed. It's a very involved process to get around in this boat; this keeps me focused.

Sometimes too focused! Wet gash is disgusting if you're feeling a little seasick. It gets emptied after each meal by a molly. The unlucky molly has to tie a knot in the bag which means getting right in close to it so you can smell it, then drag/carry it up to the weather decks all the way aft to the quarterdeck, then slit the bag open with their knife and dump the contents of the bag off the back of the boat into the ocean. Depending on the wind you have to be careful you don't end up getting splattered with food scraps. The emptied bag is then taken to the dry gash compartment to be melted down with the rest of the plastic gash. No plastic is thrown overboard by the Navy. Instead it's stacked in towers against the bulkhead in the dry gash compartment as melted down plastic pucks.

I still only sleep for a few hours at a time. The ship's motion keeps waking me up as well as the sound of the door opening and closing. The false bulkhead shakes whenever the door opens or closes, which shakes my rack which also wakes me up. Because all the women are from different departments and on different work schedules, the Mess door is constantly being opened and closed at all hours.

My favourite time is in the evening when the ship is lit in shades of deep red. Laying in my rack I feel her as she rises up over a wave, then she falls through the water with a muffled deep booming sound. There's also a gentle rhythmic swishing motion as the water rushes against the hull, and the machinery hums and drones and the bulkheads creak softly. It all combines to lull me off to sleep in a very soothing way even though I'm frequently awakened.

I'm learning that sound becomes a major consideration on-board ship. Noise discipline is strictly enforced. If you need to talk, you whisper. If you're opening your locker, you do it slowly so the metal lock doesn't make a sound against the metal of the locker. If you have loose objects like a hairbrush or batteries in the storage box at the head of your rack, they had better be wrapped in a sock. If anything begins to roll around the owner of that rack is quickly identified and told to secure their stuff at once.

No alarm clocks allowed. Instead, people get a shake by someone from their department, usually the on-watch person before them on the watch rotation who opens the rack's curtain (as little as possible of course for privacy reasons), reaches in, and shakes them awake.

The person giving the shake has usually come from a compartment using white lighting, making them night blind as they enter a room bathed in dark-red light. Consequently, it's not always possible to see, which often results in other body parts being groped accidentally. A hastily whispered apology follows, and some laughs are had about it. Some men are so afraid when they have to wake a woman that they shake her feet instead. I find a foot shake to be a cold and impersonal way to start the day.

MY FIRST BONG-BONGS

My first bong-bongs prove to be a clusterfuck. Bong-bongs refers to the sound of the general alarm as it blares throughout the ship. It sounds like a loud bong-bong that's repeated four times.

When bong-bongs sound, we immediately stop what we are doing. Conversations stop in mid-sentence. Tools are put down. Everyone listens for the type of alarm. The alarm type is announced over the shincom after the bong-bongs. This one is an emergency flying stations: the Sea King needs to make a crash landing on the flight deck. The ship prepares for the possibility of a nasty jet-fuel powered explosion and fire.

I report to my section base, falling into a steady flow of human traffic walking briskly through the flats to where they are supposed to be. As I head forward up to two deck, it's crowded with people in various stages of dressing in bunker gear (firefighting gear). No one seems to notice me but I figure I'm also supposed to get dressed. Grabbing the last set of unused bunker gear, I start to climb into it.

I did my DC school (Damage Control) training a few months ago. Dressing quickly in bunker gear was part of my training. At the DC school, everyone was individually sized so that the appropriately sized gear was given to them. We are even issued plastic wallet cards with our mask size on it. I fit a size small. What I'm climbing into is a size XL. The boots are twice the size of my feet. The mask I quickly pull over my head is an L. Following the procedure to get suction on the mask so that there's an airtight seal around my mouth and nose, I find I can't get a good seal. Before I can object, two people are hoisting a compressed-air bottle (referred to by their brand name Dräger) onto my back; I automatically cinch the straps down to fit me. The straps end up all twisted and the people helping me dress have to undo them and straighten them out. I fiddle with my mask, still unable to get a good seal.

"Let's go, let's go!" yells PO 2 Haro who is overseeing things with a clipboard and a headset. He's looking specifically at me. I'm the last person to get dressed. I clip my regulator to my mask and check my air supply on the gauge. To my surprise, the bottle is only half full. It's very hard to communicate verbally wearing full bunker gear, so I tap the shoulder of one of the guys who is helping me get suited up, then I point to my pressure gauge. He notices, and they have me bend over while they unscrew the bottle from the harness and attach a new one. By now every other sentry and attack team (the people dressed in bunker gear) have left the base. The senior NCOs watch disapprovingly as precious seconds are wasted while my bottle gets switched out.

Finally my new bottle is in place, and the pressure gauge reads full. I stumble awkwardly through the ship like the abominable snowman. This better just be a drill, I think to myself as I still can't get my mask to seal. Walking into a fire with a leaky mask means certain death from smoke inhalation. I learned in DC school that two lungs-full of burning ship smoke is enough to kill you since there are so many toxic chemicals used in the building materials.

Finally arriving at the fire boundary, a PO tells me to set up a boundary in Two-Kilo starboard side. I have no idea where Two-Kilo is except the theoretical knowledge of how deck and section numbers are laid out on ship which I remember from DC school. I try to think through it, asking for clarification from someone while I stumble around lost. That someone tells me disapprovingly that I should know where Two-Kilo is, as if this wasn't my very first bong-bongs. As if I had been present for the workups the rest of the crew took part in shortly before the deployment while I was still finishing up my trade training.

Desperate, I stumble around until finally I find Two-Kilo. It's a Mess in the aft part of the ship. But, again, I'm instantly confused and disoriented. A PO overseeing the boundaries points upward to a red painted emergency escape hatch in the deckhead. This, apparently, is where I'm supposed to set up a fire boundary. I climb up the tiny metal rung ladder attached to the bulkhead, my toes not even reaching the metal rungs because the boots are so big. Marvelling at how unsafe this whole thing is, I reach up and try to turn the wheel which is supposed to open the escape hatch so we don't die a horrible fiery death.

The wheel won't budge. I strain with all my might to turn the damn thing. The ship rolls suddenly and I almost fall. I grab at the ladder. It's a good two-metre drop to the deck below me. Afraid to fall, I continue to try to open the hatch with one hand. I'm sweating, breathing hard, swearing at the effort. If it's my job to open the escape hatch, I guess we're all dead. I'm not strong enough to do it.

The PO is watching. Finally he sighs heavily with disapproval, then gestures for me to get out of the way. I climb down quickly. He climbs up, gives the wheel a manly heave, grunting with the effort. There's a wrenching metal sound, and the hatch pops open. Once again, I curse my size. I work out harder than most men, but the laziest fattest man is still stronger than I am.

Now that the hatch is open, I see the fire hose coiled up against the bulkhead. In the training scenarios there wasn't enough time for everyone to handle the hoses. Someone else had to set up the Kingston coil, laid out in a circular fashion to save space.

Stopping a passing DC roundsman, I gesture for help with the hose. He shows me the lever to pull and how to snake out the hose. I crack the fire main. Water begins to fill the hose. Picking up the business end of the hose, I am finally ready as a sentry. I look around for the nearest shincom to report back to the section base that I'm closed up. The roundsman tells me the shincom is broken in this area, and he offers to act as a runner for me.

The XO, in charge of damage control, gets on the pipe and informs the ship that all boundaries except Two-Kilo are in place. I stand there with a charged fire hose, in position, wondering what happened to my runner. Now the whole ship thinks I'm not ready. Frustrated and awkward, I stand around until the exercise is ended. The XO never amends his pipe.

What a complete fuck-up! Having just completed Basic Training, I was placed as a boundary by myself. In Basic it's drilled into us that everything is done in at least teams of two. I failed one of my training scenarios because I sent someone off to do a job alone.

At the debrief, as we peel off layers of sweaty bunker gear, bottles of water are passed around in the section bases. Our official reaction time is calculated at just over four minutes, making the scenario a success. Close-up time is NATO standard six minutes or less. Once all the sets of bunker gear are stowed properly, I check them all. All are either L or XL.

Cautiously, I approach PO 2 Haro as he is stowing his clipboard and headset.

"Excuse me, PO. The bunker gear doesn't fit me at all. I can't get a good seal on the mask, I fit a small—"

PO 2 Haro interrupts me. "It's your job to get dressed just like all the others! Stop complaining, Ordinary Seaman." He doesn't even look at me as he continues to stow his equipment.

Speechless, I stand there for a moment. Fear rises inside me. I don't know what to say so I turn, walk awkwardly back to the shelf with the bunker gear and continue to help square things away.

Alders finds me after the debrief to talk to me.

"Peffers, you need to get dressed faster." She drives her closed fist into her palm to hammer home the point. "And you should know how to do a Kingston coil." Another fist in palm. "And you should know the layout of the ship." Another fist in palm. Her tone is very serious.

"In DC School I never—"

"And you really need to stop talking back to your superiors," Alders interrupts me. Her voice is cold, her eyes even colder. "This is a problem for you. What I need to hear is a 'Yes, Leading Seaman.' PO 1 Davin has already complained about your talking back to him. People have started to notice your behaviour." Alders pauses and crosses her arms in front of her chest as if to add emphasis to what she's about to say next: "We're disappointed with your behaviour."

I stand there as guilt, failure, and frustration well up inside me. I blink a few times in silence, unable to express these feelings. They swarm, trapped inside me.

"Yes, Leading Seaman."

For the rest of the day I work as a dishwasher while I think back again and again about the exercise. Broken shincoms, escape hatches I can't open, bunker gear dangerously too big for me, and the prevailing opinion that I'm disappointing people. This isn't what I thought the Navy would be. It's not at all like DC school. Nobody cares about my safety or that I'm so very new to the ship. I had expected a real NATO deployment would be the time when every effort would be taken to make sure people had the right gear. I didn't have the right gear, and nobody cared.

WEATHER DECKS

I start missing the sky. I've never stayed in a place with no windows or natural light. Every few days I find fifteen or twenty minutes of free time during daylight hours to go above decks. This is the one place on ship with windows and natural light. Something odd happens. I start feeling nausea when I see the horizon pitching up and down, side to side. I go below decks, and this feeling goes away. Some people refer to this as reverse seasickness. It's common among the engineering types who never see the light of day.

On the bridge, I've started leaning against a pole that's behind the nav comm station on the port side. Leaning is something that develops as a habit in the Navy. In Basic Training we weren't allowed to lean, except for the instructors who had Navy backgrounds who were subconsciously leaning all the time. They were constantly having to catch themselves. Leaning gives you three points of contact and allows both your hands to be free. It makes perfect sense.

My shoulder leans on the pole, and my head rests on its cold metal. I chat with the nav comms, who all seem to share my taste in sci-fi. I watch the rest of the bridge people. The bosuns are at the helm and propulsion, laughing at each other's dirty jokes. The officers of the watch are young, tense, and nervous. The presence of the CO and XO is calm and confident. There's a steady stream of navigation commands, random alarm noises that I don't recognize, and casual chat. When the officer of the watch isn't busy they'll give me an update on our location and heading. It feels good to know where we're going. We are a few weeks away from our next port: Okinawa, Japan.

Sometimes I visit the bridge at night. It's very dark with minimal red lighting. It's so dark that even the green glow from the instruments is dimmed. It's so dark I can't recognize anyone. We're all dark, anonymous people-shaped objects. I get to know people by the sounds of their voices.

The ocean at night is spectacular. We are completely dark at night except for our port and starboard running lights, masthead steaming light, and stern light. The result is that the view of the sky and ocean is amazingly clear. I walk out onto the port bridge wing, look up, and my jaw drops in amazement. The Milky Way streaks clearly across the night sky. I can see more stars now than I've ever seen before. The sky is dense with points of light. The starlight makes the sky lighter than the ocean. In contrast, the ocean is a dull black except when the moon is out, glistening on the water.

OS Merrit, the port lookout, comes up to me.

"You seasick?"

"Nah, just looking at the stars."

He hands me a pair of night-vision goggles. "Check out the stars now."

Raising the goggles to my eyes, I look up again. This time the sky is lit up in a bright, sonic-green colour. There are so many points of white light that they bleed together. The sky is densely packed with stars. A shiver runs down my spine as I take in the experience. After saying "wow" many times I hand back the goggles. OS Merrit laughs.

One night after dumping the wet gash, a small group of firefighters and air det accumulate on the quarterdeck, which is the end of the ship, around the bollards. They start chatting and smoking. I stop to listen in. A firefighter called Starch explains earnestly to anyone who'll listen that aliens are completely plausible in our universe. I sit with the small audience to hear him out. He gestures up to the night sky, at all the countless millions of stars up there, and tells us that statistically there must be someone else out there.

The conversation moves on to space travel and how the Navy is the closest thing to replicating the kind of isolation that space travel would have. We are days away from the nearest port. There are kilometres of water under us. We are completely alone out here. I look up at the stars while I listen. It's almost like we're in space right now. I see the black outline of the hangar and all the communications equipment sprouting from above the bridge along with the mast. Black outlines of antennas and satellite dishes. If you ignore the water, it looks like we're a spaceship in space.

I grin in the darkness. The conversation is welcomed distraction from the troubles I'm having with my superiors. I feel a sense of belonging while we sit under the best view of the stars on the planet, talking about space with each other.

One day when I have a split shift (early morning then late night in the Cave), I climb up and out of the ship and sit on a bollard on the quarterdeck alone. Sitting, I watch our wake from the props. The sky is overcast, and the water is grey. It matches my mood after once again being singled out and yelled at by Davin. I can't seem to do anything right for him. It's then that a sudden homesickness hits me. I miss my boyfriend, Roy, waiting for me in Edmonton. We spent a year and a half apart while I went through all my military training. He plans to move out to the Island for our homecoming date of August twenty-first. A wave of loneliness consumes me, and I start crying, alone on the quarterdeck.

OS Simon approaches me.

"Can I join you?" he asks gently.

I nod wordlessly, wiping my eyes on my uniform sleeve. Simon sits next to me. "I saw you sitting here all by yourself, you look sad."

"Yeah, I'm homesick," I say, sniffing.

We sit in silence together on our bollards for a while. We both went through Basic Training together, and now through a complete coincidence we're both on the same boat doing the same deployment.

"The rumour mill says you have a bad attitude," Simon says, breaking the silence.

"Gee, thanks for cheering me up."

"I don't believe it." He turns to look at me from his bollard. "You're a good person. You just need some time to adjust to being on ship."

I wipe the last of the tears from my eyes.

"Take me for example," he goes on. "When I first got to the boat, I was constantly in trouble. Couldn't do anything right." Simon looks out to sea then. "My first day on ship, my shop master seaman tells me to go get fifty yards of shoreline. I says, 'Yes, Master Seaman!' and went off to rope stores to look. I looked and looked but couldn't find any. After a few hours of looking, a leading seaman came to find me and tell me that shoreline doesn't exist. That it was a joke."

I laugh. Simon smiles and chuckles quietly.

"Check out the horizon," Simon points and I follow his finger.

I see what looks like land in the distance, and I'm suddenly disoriented. I thought we were days away from land.

"It's an optical illusion," Simon explains. "It's the shadow of clouds in the distance, but it looks like land."

"Neat," I say, a little disconcerted. I have a blind faith in the navigational skills of the bridge officers, trusting they are getting us where we need to be.

"We're a long ways away," Simon takes out his knife and flicks it open casually. "But we're not alone."

"No? How so?"

Simon points with his knife to the quarterdeck. I follow his gesture and I see a large, white bird swerving a lazy figure eight behind us.

"It's an albatross, been following us since Hawaii," Simon smiles. "It's considered good luck."

I smile too, my sadness forgotten.

WEATHER WITCH

One day while on the bridge, I bump into Jed while he relays some info to the officer of the watch.

"Hey, Peff, nice to see you up here. Most engineering types tend to stay below decks. This is a pleasant surprise, seeing you out and about."

"I like to see what's going on, plus the windows."

"Here, come with me," Jed walks aft through the doorway leading out of the bridge and into the bridge flats. I follow him. He makes a sharp left into the chart room and sits down at a desk with a laptop and a pair of small speakers playing soft rock music. He spreads his arms wide, a gesture to encompass the entire compartment. "This is where I work. Welcome, welcome!"

There's a large chart table and a few chairs in the cramped space. I ignore the spare chair and hoist myself up onto the chart table, my legs dangling against the chart drawers. I look around and see the Chinese character for serenity printed on a piece of paper taped above the computer screen. Jed flips through some screens on his laptop.

"See, these are the meteorological charts for this area of the world."

I lean over to get a better look from my vantage point atop the chart table. "Neat."

"So," Jed swivels in his chair to face me. "How do you like being molly?"

I nod, pressing my lips together. "It's okay."

Jed laughs.

"Come on, tell me what you really think."

"I…" I don't want to complain.

"Come on Peff, everyone hates being molly. It's okay to admit it."

"Okay, I admit it, it kinda sucks." I smile then.

"Everybody complains about being molly," Jed assures me. "When JD was molly just before you, he didn't stop bitching about it." Jed wags his finger then to prove a point. "It's every sailor's lot in life to complain about the job that they've been given."

"Oh, really?" I laugh.

"That's how the higher-ups know things are going well. If the men aren't complaining about something then there's something wrong." Jed leans back in his chair thoughtfully. "Take me for example." He gestures to his computer. "All I have to do is gather the data for a morning weather report and watch for storms on the horizon. That's it. For twelve straight hours a day." He pauses then, sighing heavily. "Hence the music. It takes me maybe two hours to do my job each day. The rest of the time I'm just sitting. Of course I have to be here in case there's a freak storm, but the chances of that…" Jed trails off, then looks at his computer monitor again. "Sometimes I play solitaire," he says dryly.

I laugh again. I'm really warming up to Jed.

"I have to go soon, gotta go be molly again."

"You're welcome back here anytime. You won't be interrupting anything. If I'm gone then just hang around because I'll be back soon. I'm never gone long. I'm chained to this compartment. Chained, I tell you."

"Thanks, I think I'll be back then." I smile and hop down from the chart table.

"Anytime you want a break from things…"

"Okay," I wave goodbye and leave the compartment to head back down below. I find Jed's company to be very pleasant. I think I'm starting to make some real friends on-board.

CBRN TRAINING

CBRN stands for Chemical Biological Radiological Nuclear; we train to survive and fight in these conditions. We have what's called a citadel enclosing our working and living spaces. Airlocks are required to enter or leave the citadel. They're airtight and watertight (in theory anyway) and maintain a positive air pressure compared to outside. Special CBRN filters let only 10 per cent fresh air in while recycling 90 per cent of all other air. The filters can close completely, so recycled air allows us to sail through a cloud of anthrax essentially unharmed (in theory). Ninety per cent recycled air spreads airborne illness very effectively as well.

Word comes down the chain that we are going to carry out CBRN drills in preparation for being sent to the Box, a war zone where a ship is deployed. Everyone in my department is issued a CBRN suit and we're told to dig out our gas masks and flash gear. All over the ship people carry out their daily duties wearing an army-green belt with army-green pouches for the army-green suit and gloves. Army-green gas masks are strapped to people's hips as well.

Drills are carried out randomly throughout the day. Bong-bongs are heard followed by the pipe for CBRN attack. I put down the pile of plates and get dressed in my suit as quickly as possible. Dress first then move. After what feels like long minutes struggling into my suit (which is of course way too big for me), I throw my glasses from my face and slip my gas mask over my head, making the seal around my face. I'm jostled by a crowd of army-green CBRN people heading to their section bases while I grope around on the deck to find my glasses. I accept that if I'm ever in a real deadly gas attack, that extra second it takes to remove my glasses might be the difference between living and dying. After a few seconds of groping, I find my glasses and put them in the breast pocket of my suit. My world has turned blurry. I head briskly to the forward section base where a PO 2 with a clipboard and a headset is taking attendance. Everyone has to yell to be heard, talking with their masks on.

Once everyone is present and accounted for, duties are assigned. I'm assigned as a hatch sentry up forward for the hatch that I first used to climb inside *Winnipeg* back in Hawaii. I breathe a sigh of relief because this time I actually know where I'm going. We're given a handful of test strips to use around the doors and hatches to ensure a good seal is kept.

Spending the next few hours closed up in sweaty CBRN gear, guarding my hatch and periodically sticking test strips around the seal, I think my hatch is leaking because I can hear a hissing noise. I report this to all the POs who check up on me every half hour. Depending on the person, replies vary from assuring me that that's normal to telling me they'll report it to the MCR right away. I'm confused and unsettled by this.

All the while the ship steers a zigzag pattern through the water from port to starboard and back again. The heavy manoeuvres act like a heavier sea state as we roll fifteen degrees to port then fifteen degrees to starboard. The motion makes me drowsy. The zigzag pattern is part of the CBRN manoeuvres as well as a pre-wet sprinkler system that sprays a mist of sea water on every weather deck. This would help rinse away nuclear fallout particles or chemicals. The zigzag is necessary to ensure the spray drains from the surfaces of the ship.

The XO comes on the pipe and gives us an update. We are allowed to remove our gas masks for now so we can rehydrate after all the sweating. More bottles of water are passed around.

CBRN drills continue like this for a few days. One day we're closed up in the forward section base wearing our green suits and gas masks, and we are just required to wait out. The weapons tech shop is adjacent to the forward section base so when we're sitting around in the base we spill into the weapons tech shop because they have seats, a bench, a couch strapped in way up by the deckhead, and a TV and DVD player. We all squeeze into the seats and sit on the deck waiting.

LS Lannon finds one of my romance novels; I had left it on the bench from a previous time we were closed up here. With a flourish he quickly searches through the book until he finds a juicy passage. Then, while yelling through his green gas mask so everyone can hear him, he goes about reading the passage aloud to everyone. Maybe it's the fatigue, maybe it's the way he's reading it, but having someone yell in a tinny muffled voice a sexual seduction scene is hilarious. We laugh so loud the section base PO 1 yells at us to keep it down.

Eventually the exercise is ended, and I gratefully peel off my CBRN suit. Each department takes their turn lining up at the ship's office to hand back all the army-green suits, and our gas masks and flash gear go back to wherever we happen to stash them. My department keeps theirs clipped to a pipe in the shop. There's no more room on that pipe so I keep mine in the top of my locker; this difference makes me feel left out.

Despite the mixed opinions about my hatch leaking or not, CBRN drills are considered successful and we are officially ready for the Box. All that's left is to hook up our new chemical/biological detection unit. It's supposed to take constant air samples from the weather decks, and if a known contagion or chemical weapon is detected, an alarm will sound in the MCR.

It's not long before the chemical/biological detection unit alarm sounds. After an investigation, it's decided that it's just a random false positive. The system is left alone again. Again the alarm sounds, and again. After more investigating it turns out that this million dollar machine is also triggered by diesel and paint fumes. The bosuns were painting the upper decks, and diesel fumes permeate everything on-board.

It's decided that the most practical course of action is to simply shut the system off. It's far too disruptive to have false alarms going off all the time. Again, I get that sinking feeling that we're not as tough as we think we are. No one else expresses any concern, except Jed when we discuss it in the chart room.

"Nobody seems concerned," I say while perched atop the chart table.

Jed laughs. "Yeah, that's the Navy way," he says dryly. "Just think, all our CBRN gear is stowed, not within easy reach, and we only get issued our suits if we get a warning of an attack." He pauses dramatically.

"Who warns their enemies before they attack? If anyone uses chemical weapons against the Canadian Navy we're not going to know about it until it's happening."

I sit in silence, taking in his logic.

"And then the next ship will hopefully be prepared," Jed finishes.

"So it makes more sense to carry around our gear all the time?"

"While in the Box, I'd say so." Jed pauses to shake his head. "It was what we did in Afghanistan."

WHO WILL YOU FUCK IN A FOREIGN PORT?

It's been more than two weeks at sea, and we're almost at Okinawa. When I go above decks now I see strange little fishing boats with fin-style sails. The officer of the watch tells me they are called dhows. It's strange because the ocean itself hasn't changed appearance. It still looks like we could be just off the coast of Vancouver Island. Except there are traditional Japanese fishing boats in the area.

I'm looking forward to a few days' rest when I can sleep for as long as I want. Every morning it seems to get harder to drag myself from my warm, soft rack. I've tripled my normal coffee intake.

One evening before I head aft to do my workout, I stop at the shop and find JD, Kelvin, and Dale playing music and chatting. I join them, wanting to participate in a conversation. Sitting on the counter, I listen.

"Fords are better than Chevys anyway. Why'd you buy one?" Dale is saying.

"No way man, you know what Ford stands for right? Chevys'll run forever," Kelvin replies.

"Found On Road Dead," Dale laughs.

"What about you, Peff, what kinda car d'you own?" Kelvin asks.

"I don't have a car, I have a student loan," I reply bitterly. Dale and Kelvin laugh at that. "Well, I suppose if I really wanted to I could get a beater," I shrug. "I guess I'm fine without one."

"I couldn't survive without my truck," Kelvin says.

Just then the PO 1 turns up at the door. He turns to look at me.

"OS Peffers, just what do you think you're doing?" His voice is strict.

"Oh, I was just going to do a workout," I say, uneasiness building inside me.

"Then you do your workout. You don't hang around on ship in workout gear. You don't see OS Kelvin or OS Dale wearing workout gear do you?" PO 1 sounds angry.

"I didn't know…" I haven't seen anyone else hanging out on ship out of uniform so I suppose what he's saying makes sense; I just didn't know it was a rule.

"Stop talking back, Ordinary Seaman, and stop making excuses."

Robertson pauses then, studying me.

"Where is your uniform, Ordinary Seaman?"

"Hanging at my locker…" I say, confusion starting to flow over the shame I'm feeling at doing something wrong again.

"You're supposed to have your uniform on you at all times, that includes workout times. You carry it with you. That way if there's bong-bongs you dress over your workout clothes to save time."

"Oh, I didn't know that…"

"You should know that by now, Ordinary Seaman. Go and get your uniform right now. You know, you're developing a real problem with authority figures." Robertson's voice is as hard as steel.

Without another word, I leave the shop and head forward to my locker to retrieve my uniform. I'm grateful for the red night lighting as it hides my blushing face. I bundle up the clothes and tuck my boots under my arm before heading aft again. Passing by the door to the shop I see the PO 1 standing in the doorway laughing with Kelvin and Dale. My gait falters. For a moment I'm an outsider looking in. The laughter and music waft down the flats after me. Excluded, I continue walking down the flats in search of an empty treadmill.

To make matters worse, my next time working out I forget to bring my uniform along just because it's a new thing and sometimes new things take awhile to sink in with me. I have to unlearn a habit. Of course PO 1 Robertson happens to be doing a set of rounds and sees me without my uniform.

"Ordinary Seaman Peffers, you don't have your uniform with you again. This is your last chance before reprimands start going on your record," he tells me coldly.

Guilt stabs through me as I reply, "Sorry, PO."

Something else that's been forgotten out here are weekends. The weeks go by, and it's strange to go so long without one. It slowly dawns on me that the days of the week no longer matter out here. They blur together since every day is essentially the same, everyone carrying out the same duties. There's a running joke in the Navy about the movie *Groundhog Day* and how it mirrors life while at sea. Jed tells me that when it's over and I'm home again, I won't even remember most of the sailing.

I'm hanging out in the chart room on one of my afternoon breaks a few days before we are due to arrive in Okinawa.

"So Peff, how are things?" Jed leans back in his chair and regards me at my spot on the chart table.

I dangle my legs against the chart table drawers. "Fine, I guess."

"I hear you have a bad attitude. Look out, Bad Attitude Peff is here!"

I smile nervously.

"Oh yeah, here comes trouble," Jed's voice is dripping with sarcasm. He chuckles to himself. "Yup, one ninety-pound girl is gonna be the end of this boat," he continues, laughing.

"Hey, I'm not ninety pounds, I work out!"

"You know, it's because you're smart; it threatens them, they don't like that. You can't have an independent thought at your rank." Jed pauses thoughtfully. "Every PO 1 here is a king of his own little fiefdom, and boy can they micromanage." He pauses again. "Little fiefdoms."

There's a lull in the conversation, and I take the opportunity to make a comment.

"I see you have the sign for serenity there," I point to the piece of paper taped above his monitor.

"I do, it keeps me serene…see how it's working?" Jed says with more sarcasm. He sits up straighter before continuing. "I really admire the Shinto traditions: martial arts, the discipline, and honour. Speaking of which, we're quickly approaching Okinawa."

"I know, the ocean is full of little dhows." Excitement and curiosity rise inside me.

"There's a castle and gardens tour booked by one of the officers. Would you like to come with me? That is, if you haven't already made plans."

I smile at that.

"Thank you, yes," I think maybe I've just made a real friend on-board. "Providing my molly schedule allows for it," I add.

"Excellent! Afterwards we can get drunk on sake," Jed exclaims.

There's a pause in the conversation then, and I start to wonder about Jed's motives for being so kind to me. Almost as if he read my mind, Jed continues.

"Don't worry, Peff, I'm not trying to fuck you. I know people start pairing off right about now. I've seen it just before every port on all the deployments I've done. I'm married."

"Oh, well, that's great. I have a boyfriend too, not really looking to be fucked." A sigh of relief escapes my lips as I relax again.

Tourist pamphlets for all the traditional Japanese attractions in Okinawa appear on the tables in the Cave. There are a few tours sched-uled for the ship's company, and a local bus is rented to ferry us from the ship to downtown. I'm browsing through the pamphlets, and the bong-bongs suddenly sound again. I'm instantly alert, I listen for the announcement for the kind of alarm. This one is a man overboard. I relax again. I don't respond to those since I'm part of the engineering department.

People walk quickly down the flats as I continue cleaning tables. The ship's engines drone to full speed and the deck suddenly rolls thirty degrees to starboard, and I grab a nearby counter for support. This is the Williamson turn, the fastest way to get the boat back to the position of the man in the water. The deck stays pitched over for the duration of the turn and I can hear metallic clangs from the galley as unsecured steel bowls fly off counters. The rest of the mollies and I watch risky objects in the Cave, like the mound of fruit in the fruit bowl. There's a loud crash from just behind me, and I turn to see the large coffee pot rolling on the deck, spilling a gallon of black coffee all over the place. The dark brown liquid starts to move of its own accord as the deck pitches back over again and we are upright once more.

The mollies erupt in a barrage of swearing. The pot is placed back on the counter again, and rags are quickly passed around. If Davin sees this he'll be pissed; then we'll all be in trouble. We wipe furiously at the black liquid as quickly as possible. Some of it drips behind the counters which can't be helped, but we get most of it cleaned up within a minute.

"Hey, the bungee cord is missing," Finnerty notices as she stands up again. Theft is an unfortunate reality on-board.

"I'll run to Gen Stores #1 to get another one," Coté is already heading for the door.

The coffee pot is secured to the bulkhead again, with a new bungee cord, and Davin never finds out about the spilled coffee.

The day we come alongside Okinawa, Davin calls a meeting in the Cave for all the mollies. He looks between Finnerty and myself as he explains his rule for the alongside schedule.

"Anyone who wants to get every day off while in foreign port can meet me in thirty minutes up forward in Gen Stores #1." He pauses while Finnerty and I catch the innuendo. He smiles mischievously at the both of us.

Gen Stores #1 is way up forward outside the citadel and is an unmanned compartment. It stores supplies for the cooks and mollies and is among other things one of the more private places on ship. I exchange a look with Finnerty, who laughs and rolls her eyes. I'm actually not sure if Davin's serious or joking.

Just before the boat is piped secure, PO 1 Robertson calls a meeting in the shop. Once everyone is wedged in, he starts to speak.

"The ship has rented out a campground for the night on the base here. It should be fun, there are campfires and a liquor store. You should all come out and have some fun. We've rented a camper for the night, so that's where we can hang out." Robertson pauses, then continues. "Here's hoping the giant mobs of bats stay away." He laughs then, shaking his head.

"Bats?" asks JD.

"Oh yeah," Alders pipes in. "Last trip to Okinawa, the PO was sitting at a picnic table, and a swarm of them descended upon him."

"I had to do a crazy dance to get them off me," Robertson laughs.

"And they were huge," adds Stafford, indicating with his hands, "disgusting creatures."

OKINAWA

This foreign port I have two days off, but not back-to-back. Most of the back-to-back leave days fall upon the higher ranks. For my first day off, I sleep until noon. I wake up feeling blessedly rested. I eat a casual lunch in the mostly empty Cave; then I go to the ship's office and get a pay advance in Japanese currency. Then I head up to the weather decks and cross the brow, and just like that I'm standing on Japanese soil.

Walking around the base, I admire the coastline. With some of the ship's company I take a bus into downtown Okinawa, and we buy some souvies at a large mall. Everything seems cute and cartoon-like in Japan. Even the diapers in a passing diaper commercial. Come evening, I make my way back to the base and follow a walking trail for a few minutes to the campground the ship has rented.

Sitting at a picnic table with lots of beer on it, I start drinking. Alders is there, talking to her friends. One table over, the stokers are rowdy and drunk. No one seems to notice my presence. I decide to go looking for the rest of my shop and try hanging out with them. Alders points me in the direction of our trailer.

I open the door to the trailer and walk inside. I see OS Kelvin and Dale closest to me in the middle of the trailer. There is another man sitting there as well and I see his bare torso, arms and head facing me from the opposite side of the trailer. There's a table between us. Just as a warning is going off in my head that he looks naked, Kelvin and Dale quickly leave the trailer. I'm aware of their motion peripherally, then I realize I'm alone with this naked man and he is telling me "Have a seat," in no uncertain terms.

I don't want to get in any more trouble so I walk to the table and sit across from him. He's looking at me very intensely. His gaze is studying me. He's leaning forward, his forearms on the table, nursing his beer.

I remember this image, and I remember seeing his mouth move as more and more fear rises up inside me. He's talking to me. I'm staring back at him. I feel pressure on my right foot. I feel like he's touching me. I look down and see his foot is touching my foot under the table. Definite intentional pressure. I look from his foot to his face, and he just gazes intently at me.

I'm alone and vulnerable. Not only is he much higher in rank then me, but he is also bigger and stronger.

"Move your foot, it's touching me and grossing me out," I say. I sound disgusted, then I'm afraid of getting in trouble because of my tone of voice.

He sniffs, looks away, and moves his foot so that it's no longer touching mine.

"So, I hear you're a failed officer," he tells me next.

I stare.

"What happened?" he asks in an unctuous tone of voice. I don't know what to say. I have to think quickly and speak carefully.

"During Basic Training I collapsed from exhaustion. I found out I have anemia. They gave me pills, but it takes a long time to recover. Almost at the end of my second attempt at Basic I was exhausted again so I took a recruit school bypass and became an NCM."

"I want you to understand my role in your training," he takes a sip of beer. "Everyone will be watching and judging you," he continues, his gaze still studying me. "Including me." He looks hungry as he continues to eye me. "You'll have to pass an oral board in front of your entire chain of command including the EO, and you'll have to convince everyone in the room that you are worthy of getting your watch." I'm shocked. Is he really trying to seduce me? I move my head to the left and see our reflection in the window. It's dark outside, and the window acts like a mirror. I see a table and two chairs, a man sitting in his white briefs, almost naked with a beer in his hands, very intently watching everything I do.

He leans forward and whispers, "Hey, Peffers." This gets my attention, and I turn to face him again. I can't believe his behaviour. I've already learned that I don't have the authority to tell people how to behave. I feel danger now, and I smile. I think briefly of my boyfriend waiting so patiently for me in Edmonton.

"I have to go," I say evenly.

"No you don't," he tells me.

"Yes, I do." There's a tension in my chest. I just know I have to leave this situation as soon as possible and find a group of people. That would be safe. Alone I am trapped. I've never had to sleep with anyone to succeed on the job before, and I'll be damned if I have to now.

"I need to go."

"No you don't."

"I really need to go."

"No, you don't," he tells it to me more quietly now.

"I NEED to go," I tell him.

He's been shaking his head and telling me no, but then he looks like he realizes something and laughs.

"Oh, you mean you need to GO," he says. He pushes himself away from the table. I force a smile and laugh as I stand to get up.

My hand is reaching for the doorknob while my spine is tingling. I can't move fast enough, but I don't want to appear too rushed. I don't want to encourage any kind of chasing. I don't want to show fear as I leave the trailer. Everything is very alive right now, and I'm walking away seeing the individual blades of grass below my feet.

I'm walking away. I force myself not to run from the trailer. What the hell just happened? My heart is pounding in my ears. I orient toward the sound of people's voices and see a campfire in the distance. I make a straight line for it. People are gathered around the fire, people I recognize from the engineering department. I sit on a log in front of the fire and stare into the flames and breathe. Before I can even start to process what just happened to me, Chief Correy the Chief ERA approaches me and sits beside me on the log.

He leans toward me and speaks, "You know, you'd make an old man very lucky. Sailing can be a very lonely time."

What? Again? I look at him incredulously. This is the highest-ranking senior NCO stoker in my chain of command. I have to again pick my words carefully around my superiors.

"I, um, have a boyfriend…"

"Well, it was worth a shot," Correy shrugs and goes back to his drinking buddies.

I'm surrounded by laughter and talking. I'm invisible. Doesn't anyone besides Jed want to get to know me as a friend? A definite sinking feeling is settling deep into the pit of my stomach. Shit. Oh Shit, I keep thinking. This is just the beginning of the deployment, and I've already made an enemy. It dawns on me that this is probably going to be a hard six months. I sit utterly alone. Scared.

The next day is my first time being molly while alongside in a foreign port. It sucks more than being molly while sailing. The Cave is a disaster. The ship's bar is completely open at night, not just the beer machine. A shot costs you $1.50. There was lots of drinking last night. A few people lie passed out on the black leather love seats, some in uniform, some in civvies.

Empty beer bottles and cans lay strewn around every surface. Puddles of spilled beer on the deck. On the long tables, crumbs and smears of jam and peanut butter along with leftover plates of food. On the counters, half-empty bags of bread lie open in piles, and the toaster area is packed with half-used jars of jam, peanut butter, and margarine. On closer inspection, each condiment has smears of all the other condiments in it and dirty knives lay littered about the counter. The recycling bins are overflowing,…the wet gash? Well, I don't even want to look at the wet gash. The scullery is filthy. The dishwasher, sink and garburator have an unsteady looking mountain of dirty dishes piled high on the counter and in the sink. There's a distinctly mouldy smell coming from the standing water in the dishwasher. All this from one night.

I'm still taking in the scene when Finnerty shows up for her shift with me. Finnerty shows no outward reaction and simply picks up the nearest cloth and starts wiping down placemats. At least Davin is away today. If he thought the Cave was a shit pit before, I don't know what he would call this. I go to the scullery and start draining the old dishwasher water. Finnerty and I are going to be very busy for the next few hours.

I'm finishing wiping down the cutting board in front of the toaster. All the condiments and knives have been put away. The counter is finally looking clean again. One of the guys who was passed out on one of the love seats earlier stumbles over to the neat pile of bread loaves in the corner. His face is puffy and lined where the leather was pressing against his skin. His hair is sticking up at odd angles and his clothes are wrinkled. He takes a slice of bread, shambles over to the toaster, and goes about toasting his bread while he scratches his ass. I move out of his way. He seems oblivious to my presence. I start to make a fresh pot of coffee. I watch while he takes his piece of toast out of the toaster, drops it onto the cutting board, opens up a brand new jar of peanut butter, gets a knife from the utensil rack in the flats, spreads his toast, drops the knife in the pile of crumbs, leaves the lid off the jar, takes a bite, and wanders back to the love seat, leaving a trail of crumbs behind him. What a pig, I think with disgust. I go back to the cutting board area and clean it up again.

In the afternoon we store ship. A human chain develops from the jetty where the delivery trucks are parked, all the way across the weather decks, into the CO's airlock, down into the Cave, and down farther to four deck where the fridge flats are, and finally to five deck where dry stores is. I form part of the human chain on the ladder leading to the fridge flats. I pass down boxes and boxes of fruits and veggies, fancy Japanese yoghurts, and all kinds of frozen meats. Every time a flat of carrots or cucumbers gets handed to me, the guys next to me make phallic comments.

"Hey Peff, look it's your favourite vegetable," says an OD as he passes me a box of cucumbers.

"My favourite?" I ask as I hand it to the OD next to me.

"Just the right size…for her pleasure," the OD laughs.

"Oh, right, hey wait up, I may want one of those for later!" I call down the chain.

"The box'll go straight to your rack," assures a leading seaman as he laughs.

Once I finish storing ship, I'm free. The rest of my Okinawa time is spent being a tourist. That night I can't find anyone I recognize so I take a cab into town by myself to go exploring. The cab driver speaks English with a heavy accent.

"Your husband in Navy?" he asks, looking at me through his rear-view mirror.

"No, I'm in the Navy," I say, gesturing to myself.

"Oh!" He looks surprised.

In town, I browse some shops and find a sushi restaurant where you take your shoes off at the door and a pipe pours green tea right at your table.

After I finish my sushi, I make my way back to the boat and later in the evening go up to the flight deck to meet Jed.

"Hey, Peff," Jed is sitting on a bollard. He stands up, hoisting a backpack over his shoulder. "Ready to go?"

"Absolutely," I smile. "Let's get out of here."

Jed and I get a tour of a Japanese castle and Zen gardens. I take lots of pictures, drink green tea in a tea ceremony, and true to his word, Jed finds a sake bar come evening.

"More sake?" Jed offers the small white jug up to me from across our table.

"Sake-it to me," I say, then laugh. Jed smiles while he pours. We're on our third bottle now. I feel warm and relaxed.

"Awe, Peff is drunk," Jed says endearingly.

"So are you," I take another sip of my drink.

"I have to admit, you're keeping pace with me. I'm impressed."

"Why thank you," I smile again. "I've worked hard to build this kinda tolerance."

"I remember when I was at your rank, I had a pretty high alcohol tolerance as well," Jed snorts. "It's the only way to survive all the bullshit. You know, your training PO spends most of his Turning-To time sitting on his ass in front of the TV in the chief's and PO's Mess. I know, it's my Mess."

"What's Turning-To mean again?"

"Regular 8 a.m. to 4 p.m. workday."

"Right. Well. I guess at his rank, he can manage his own time as wisely as he wants."

"The higher up you go in rank, the easier it gets."

"So rank has its privileges."

"You bet." Jed glances at his watch. "It's past midnight; we should be getting back to the boat."

"Okay," I stand to get up and the world tilts a little too far. I catch myself against the table.

Jed laughs. "You okay?" He also stands up, but he doesn't appear to have any trouble with this.

"Oh yeah, I'm fine," I wave my hand dismissively and try standing up straight again. This time I manage to find my balance.

"You have a seat," Jed points to our table. "I'll go pay the bill."

I shrug and smile lazily, "Okay." I wait a few minutes while Jed pays, then he comes back to the table.

"Now the trick is…" Jed starts to say as he reaches out a hand for me. I take it, and he pulls me to my feet again. I stumble into him by accident, dizziness consuming me for a few seconds. "You have to walk across the brow by yourself, no help from me, in order to not be too drunk."

I laugh. Jed lets go of me for a few seconds and I sway on the spot. "That's how they measure it?" I ask. "For drunk and disorderly conduct?"

Jed laughs too. "Yep. Think you'll make it?"

"Absolutely!" I say with gusto.

"That's the spirit, Peff." Jed holds the door open for me, and we walk out into the fresh night air. It's only a short walk back to the boat. True to my word, I make it across the brow all by myself.

TWO BEERS PER PERSON PER DAY PERHAPS

All of *Winnipeg*'s machinery thrums to life, and we close up for exit of harbour again. Davin comes down to the Cave and gives another nicotine-deprived, anger-filled lecture, although this time he doesn't call me girl. Breakfast is in full swing, one of the cooks yells "Molly!" down the flats, and just like that we're sailing again.

This time the sea is a bit rougher, and a general malaise settles over the ship's company. Gravol patches appear on people's necks, and the love seats are filled with seasick sleeping people. I lose my appetite as I work through the motion. This evening I sit looking at my bowl of ravioli with slight disgust.

"Oh, Peff is seasick!" JD and Kelvin laugh at me. I smile meekly. It's true I confess, I'm seasick. It's because of the rougher sea state around Japan. A rougher sea state means bigger waves and therefore more motion.

"You have to try and eat three meals a day," Alders tells me, not unkindly.

I take a few bites, start feeling sick, and stop. Stafford has already finished his and offers to eat mine as well. We all watch in amazement at how much Stafford can eat, especially with this sea state. He tells us between bites that rough seas are the best opportunity to stuff yourself because so many people aren't eating.

The next day I show up for work tired, cold, and physically weak. I stagger to the nearest love seat and collapse shivering onto the plush leather. My body feels like a ton of lead weights. My last act is to grab the grey wool fire blanket from the back of the seat and pull it over me. Dizziness consumes me, and I fall asleep almost instantly. I'm semi-conscious and hear Davin's voice in the background. He's asking where I am. I hear JD tell him I'm seasick and to just let me sleep. JD is my hero, and I fall back into a weirdly deep sleep.

I wake up in the afternoon and see that I've joined the ranks of the fallen. All around me are unconscious bodies on sofas. I'm feeling less weak now, so I get up and continue being molly. I'm relieved because I don't seem to be in trouble.

The time warp happens again, and the days repeat themselves. There are no more weeks or months, there is only a four-day schedule that repeats itself until we get to land again. We are in limbo.

One of my souvies from Okinawa is a small cube-shaped speaker that plugs into an MP3 player. I get some zap straps from the shop and secure it to the bulkhead in the scullery. I plug it in and connect my iPod, and now I can listen to music as I wash dishes. The first song I play is "In the Navy" by the Village People. It gets smiles on people's faces. It's not long before the other mollies are plugging in their own MP3 players when they're working. I think it's always better to work to music. The cube is a hit. It's not long before the cooks tell us there are noise complaints, and we have to keep the volume down.

Robertson holds a meeting in the shop, and I'm told to attend. Everyone except Holloway, who is on watch, squishes into the tiny shop again.

"Welcome back to more sailing. For this leg of the journey, the watch rotation is posted on the back of the door," Robertson gestures to the door.

"Please familiarize yourself with your own schedules. Now, OS Peffers, I have two new training opportunities for you. You will be in charge of the cathodics reports, and you'll be the RAS ET. The guys will take turns training you up on the RAS procedures, then once the RAS buffer is confident in your abilities, you will carry out RAS procedures alone." Robertson pauses and glances at me before continuing, his arms crossed in front of his chest. "I expect you to work extra hard now because you still have all your training packages to complete on time. You have just under five months left."

Robertson pauses again before continuing. "Our next port will be Busan, South Korea. OS Peffers will be added to the watch rotation as a double-banked watchkeeper when we slip. OS Peffers, you will be doing one-in-four Turning-To. In the meantime I expect you to get along with Davin as molly. I don't want to hear about anymore talking back."

"Yes, PO."

Robertson continues, "The faster you can get trained up, OS Peffers, the faster we have another watchkeeper and the more sleep we can all get."

"Yes, PO," I say again. My gaze falls to the deck as I feel the burden of deadlines hovering over me.

I wonder why the other ODs don't have as much work as I do. The only other person in the entire shop who has a secondary duty is LS Stafford who manages the ET Stores. All the rest of them have to do is show up, do rounds, and socialize.

During one of my visits to the bridge I hug my pole while the officer of the watch tells me where we are, which is somewhere in the East China Sea. I feel the familiar cold metal on my temple as I rest my head against her. I am a turtle carrying its home on its back. We all are. The boat is home, but home goes all over the world.

KNOW YOUR SHIT

I'm ordered into the shop again by Robertson.

"Ordinary Seaman Peffers," Alders starts to say as Robertson closes the door to the shop. Her tone of voice is serious, and I already have a sinking feeling again. "It's been brought to our attention that you've altered the wording on the cover of your *Know Your Ship* booklet to read Know Your Shit."

I had thought it would be funny. Instantly I realize how wrong I was. Guilt wells up inside me as I say, "It was a joke…"

"It's not funny, this is serious," Alders continues. "This is behaviour unbecoming of an ordinary seaman and I am ordering you to fix it immediately."

It's then that I see the bottle of whiteout on the counter. Alders picks it up and hands it to me. "Fix it now," she orders.

"Yes, Leading Seaman," I mumble as I rummage in my drawer to get my booklet. She stands over me while I apply the whiteout and write a large "p" in felt pen over top of it.

I was just trying to get a laugh. It seems I can't even do that right. Awash with a heavy layer of guilt, I'm let out into the flats again.

"How's your training going?" Alders asks me from the sink next to mine. I'm in Head and Wash Place #2, up forward close to where we both sleep. I glance over, washing my hands. "Good."

"How do you like it so far, on ship?" She leans into her mirror, gently reapplying a layer of black eyeliner to her already perfect eyes.

"It's fine," I say uneasily. I'm confused because she seems genuinely interested in talking to me. Not more than a few hours ago she had reprimanded me in the shop.

Is she no longer angry with me, standing in front of her mirror? She's smiling now as she continues to talk. I feel awkwardness and confusion on top of the already present guilt from the reprimand.

She does this a lot, standing at the sink wearing only a bra and black combat pants. She has an attractive, muscular figure, and I try not to stare. I try not to notice her toned muscles under her smooth skin…

I dry my hands on my towel. She's applying layer upon layer of perfect black mascara now. I'm transfixed as she turns and smiles at me, talking again. Her new eyes pierce right through me like cool glacier-blue tunnels perfectly outlined in thick perfectly separated large black lashes. Perfect. Her eyes and face and hair are always perfect.

"Hey, Peff, don't forget you're on Mess duty tonight," she finishes as she slips out of the Heads.

KNOW YOUR SHIP

One day a large map of the world appears taped to the bulkhead in the flats along three deck. Someone has taken a marker and drawn our progress across the globe. I follow the lines from Vancouver Island to Hawaii to Japan to the middle of the East China Sea. Over the days, the map gets continuously updated.

While learning about the weather decks with my *Know Your Ship* booklet (now with a glob of whiteout over the markered-in "t" at the end of ship) I find my new favourite hangout place, the port missile deck. It's directly above the port boat deck where everyone hangs out. The port boat deck is the closest weather deck to the CO's airlock, so it's a popular place to have a quick smoke. The port missile deck takes me up and away from the crowd and gives me a better view of the whole ship.

Seeking some alone time, I sit on the catwalk stairs on the missile deck with my back to the hull. No one bothers me. It's sunny, and I watch *Winnipeg* buck over the waves while I listen to my iPod: Kings of Leon, the energetic song "Sex On Fire." Sun, my favourite music, and the motion combine to fill me with joy. I mean, look where I am and what I'm doing! I have a moment where I feel completely at home.

Part of being at home means socializing, spending time outside of work. We start to have barbeques (called banyans) on the flight deck, as a chance for the crew to relax and socialize together.

The banyans are held once a week. At least someone on-board is keeping track of the weeks. The cooks and mollies bring mounds of hamburger patties and buns up to the flight deck. Collapsible tables are brought out, and BBQs appear near the quarterdeck. The firefighters laugh and tell us the BBQs are being lit with jet fuel. Huge plastic buckets full of ice appear bulging with cans of beer and pop. People crowd onto the flight deck and quarterdeck to eat, drink, and socialize while the sun sets.

Stepping over the hatch coaming onto the flight deck, I stand in front of a busy crowd of people I don't know. A heavy feeling of isolation descends upon me as I stand there, watching the rest of the crew talk amongst themselves. People are laughing and smiling. No one notices me standing there. No one acknowledges my presence. A stab of loneliness hits my heart. Feeling a sad isolation congealing around me, I stand and watch.

I drink my beer and sit on a bollard, watching an absolutely breathtaking sunset sky turn purple on the horizon. Jed appears by my side holding a Corona.

"Hello," he says simply.

Relief floods through me. Hey I'm glad you're here, I think. We sit next to each other in a comfortable silence, watching the scene. I spy my shop through the crowd hanging out on the quarterdeck.

Jed moves on to go chat with the new junior met tech, and I head over to where my department is. There's a tired discussion under way between the ETOWs.

"If we just change it anyway and don't tell him, he won't find out," JD is saying.

"Yeah, but what about rounds?" Holloway interjects.

"We continue to do them every four hours…sure it'll be a little weird doing rounds in the middle of a watch, but this way we get more sleep," JD continues.

"We could all use more sleep," Kelvin says, rubbing his eyes.

"One-in-three Turning-To is burning you guys out," agrees Alders.

I remember learning about the watch rotations during my seamanship training course. One-in-three Turning-To is supposed to be illegal, even by Navy standards.

"You guys are standing one-in-three Turning-To?" I ask incredulously.

Everyone nods silently.

"Why?"

"It's Robertson," Alders explains, "he's gunning for his chief's promotion."

"And less sleep," JD adds bitterly. "Seriously guys, six hours on twelve off is exactly what we need, we can keep it just between the ETOWs. Nobody else has to know. So long as rounds are done every four hours, the Senior ET has no reason to be suspicious," JD says.

"Instead of going behind someone's back about it, why not just report the PO 1 to the chief ERA or EO for giving you guys an illegal watch rotation?" I ask.

A collective groan rises from the group.

"That's a terrible idea, Peff," Dale says.

"Yeah, he'll end up hating all of us for getting him in trouble," agrees Alders. "You don't want to be on the PO 1's bad side, trust me."

"Yeah, he makes the people he likes look great, and the people he doesn't like look terrible," says Stafford.

Once again I don't know what to say.

I heard the same advice from one of my instructors when they found out I was going to be working under Robertson. Appearances are all you have in the military because no one gets fired. Looking good is paramount. Doing your job well is a close second. Friends are promoted, and feuds breed infighting and bitterness.

Taking advantage of the pause in the conversation, I pull out my *Know Your Ship* booklet to do some quick studying, and Kelvin notices.

"Hey, Peff," Kelvin starts. "I dare you to go up to the CO and get something signed off by him personally."

CO stands for commanding officer, or the captain. I was working on an easy category in the booklet anyway, the location of all the stretchers on-board. I scan the flight deck until I see a small group of brass huddled together over by one of the BBQs.

"Okay!" My legs make a beeline for the highest ranking person on the boat, the one with the most stripes on their shoulders. I pause just outside the circle of brass and wait politely for a gap in the conversation. A few seconds go by, and I see my opportunity to jump in.

"Excuse me, sir," I say, looking up at the CO. He makes a show of looking mildly surprised and smiles at me from behind his sunglasses.

"Yes, Ordinary Seaman?"

"I was told you could sign off a category for my *Know Your Ship* book, I'd like to do the stretcher locations," I say, a little intimidated but determined.

"All right, let's hear it then," the CO says in a businesslike tone of voice.

I rattle off all the locations from memory in quick succession, then I hold my booklet out to him with my pen from my breast pocket for him to sign.

"Excellent work, Ordinary Seaman," the CO sounds impressed. He hands his drink to the XO standing next to him, takes my booklet and signs his initials.

"Thank you, sir." I take back my booklet and pen and head back to the quarterdeck where all the ETOWs are watching.

Kelvin gives me a high five and I hear plenty of "Holy shit, Peff!" and "She actually did it!" Most ODs are so intimidated by the rank of a CO that they wouldn't normally approach their captain.

After one banyan where I consumed my two beer maximum (two beers per day per man perhaps), I climb up to the bridge now darkened after sunset. Race Car is on the helm. Her name is LS Aston, but her nickname is Race Car. I want to sign off my "take the helm" section of the seamanship booklet.

"Hi, LS Aston," I stand behind her chair.

"Oh, you can call me Race Car," she waves her arm dismissively.

"Oh, okay, um, Race Car, can I practice taking the helm for my seamanship booklet? Maybe get it signed off?"

"Sure, have a seat." Race Car gets up from her chair and motions for me to sit down. I sit down and take in the console in front of me full of buttons and indicating dials.

Race Car carries out a ritualized dialogue with the officer of the watch to inform them that I will be taking the helm for the next half hour. I hear the officer of the watch respond with a "very good."

Taking the yoke in my hands, I follow Race Car's explanations about what all the buttons do and what all the dials indicate. After the brief I'm left sitting in the darkened bridge with the yoke in my hands; I'm doing it, I'm steering the ship! I think of driving then and remember my two beers.

"Um, I had two beers at the banyan; am I allowed to be steering a frigate?"

"It's okay, just don't make a habit of it," Race Car says.

New orders are given for a course correction by the officer of the watch and I respond appropriately and make the changes at the helm. Almost instantly *Winnipeg* starts bucking around. I don't understand; I followed the orders exactly.

"Woah, I don't..." I start to say.

"It's all right, I've got it," Race Car says as she leans over me and grabs the yoke over my own hands. She makes a subtle correction by a few degrees, and *Winnipeg* calms down again.

"Thanks," I say.

"You're welcome," Her voice is warm. "How are your training packages coming along?"

"Good, I'm working hard," I say.

"That's good, you'll get your watch in no time then."

An easy lull falls between us for a while as I sit and hold the yolk in my hands, monitoring our heading. The OOW gives new navigation commands again, and I answer those commands using proper protocols and then turn the yoke until the ship is at its new heading. *Winnipeg* starts rolling and bucking again. Race Car takes the controls and *Winnipeg* smooths right out again. Race Car seems to know how to make small adjustments a few degrees here and there to compensate. Everyone says Race Car gives us our smoothest ride whenever she's at the helm.

"You're really good at keeping the ship sailing smoothly," I comment.

"It's just experience. You get a feel for her after a while. As a member of the engineering department, you'll hardly ever be called upon to take the helm—so I wouldn't worry about it."

"So this is it huh? Better take it all in," I laugh lightly.

More silence for a while then Race Car pipes up again, "I noticed you haven't sewn your badge onto your jacket yet."

It's true, my jacket is badgeless. The ship's crest badges are still sitting in my locker.

"Yeah, I've been meaning to get around to that."

"You should probably get it done sooner rather than later; you've been on-board for more than a few weeks now. I'm sure you don't want to get into any more trouble."

"I know…it's just I've been so busy with everything."

"Tell you what…I have access to a sewing machine in the bosun's workshop; I can have them sewn onto your jackets in a matter of minutes."

"That would be really nice of you, thanks!"

"Don't mention it. Come find me tomorrow after the Forenoon watch; I have some free time then."

"Sure, okay." Someone's helping me! I think to myself as I continue to sit at the helm. Bolstered by this new development, I feel joy again at what I'm doing. Pure exhilaration floods through me. I mean, I'm steering a frigate! It's not every day you get to do that.

Taking the helm for half an hour goes by too quickly, and before I know it I'm giving Race Car back her seat, thanking her for all her help, and watching while she signs off on that part of my *Know Your Ship* booklet. The next morning it's back to being molly again.

One day while rinsing an endless stream of dirty plates on their way to the dishwasher, a plate slips from my hand. I fumble to grab it as it shatters in the sink. A shard from the plate slices open my left middle finger. It looks deep. Blood wells up and starts to run down my hand. I put pressure on it, walk over to LS Chester, and tell him I'm going to sick bay. It's a short walk up a ladder and along the flats on two deck, but it's awkward without the use of my hands. Everyone passing me asks if I need help. I thank them but I'm practically there already.

As soon as I step into sick bay the baby doc ushers me over to the sink. I remember her from the food court in Hawaii. My cut is cleaned, sterilized, sealed closed with steri-strips, and then a bandage is applied to it.

"You're lucky it doesn't need stitches," baby doc tells me as she dries her hands on a towel. "Be sure to keep it dry now…well, you're molly so keep it as dry as possible. Come back every few days so I can check on it too, okay?"

"Okay," I say as I look around. Sick bay is full of humour. On the bulkhead is a large chocolate bar with a sign saying Emergency Chocolate Supply as well as a big red Easy Button that's been reprogrammed with rude comments. I press it, and the recording says, "I regret to inform you that you are shit out of luck."

I chuckle to myself at the recording. "That's hilarious," I comment.

"Yeah, the rest of the crew gets a good laugh out of it too," WO Lyall, the doc on-board, says while he sits at the computer filling in the report.

"You're fine, you can go back to your duties now," he tells me.

All this takes place in under fifteen minutes. Before I know it, I'm standing in the scullery rinsing plates again.

I can't wait for my shift as molly to be over so I can go visit with Jed again. Finally, I'm in the chart room with Jed. He keeps me up to date on all the good rumours.

"I got injured in the line of duty," I tell him from the chart table, holding up my bandaged finger for inspection.

"Oh you're bound to get a medal for that," Jed says dryly as he chuckles. "Injured in the line of duty! That's it, send'er home," Jed pauses. "How did it happen?"

"Ah, I was just washing dishes, and one fell from my hand and smashed in the sink. A shard sliced my finger open. Baby doc says I'm lucky it doesn't need stitches."

"Well, yours is not the only battle wound on HMCS *Winnipeg*. Injuries are on the rise throughout the crew."

"Really, why is that?"

"Doc thinks it's sleep dep. It happens every tour. People get tired, mistakes happen. Just before you arrived on the boat, a leading seaman impaled his arm on a jagged piece of steel against the bulkhead while going down a ladder. Ship hit a random wave and he flailed and wham! Skewered himself in the arm."

"Really? Wow."

"Oh, and OS Simon had a hatch fall on his head when the spring that supports its weight gave out."

"That sounds painful... is he all right?"

"Just a minor concussion... he got some rack time for it though. Oh, and that's not to mention all the people who got drunk in Okinawa and fell down ladders," Jed laughs then.

"Ouch," I laugh too.

"Oh yeah, a warship is a very unforgiving environment. Everything is either hard or sharp and pointy. Just you wait until you're on the watch rotation, you're in for a circadian treat. They make zombies out of you. Makes people prone to injuries."

Except for my finger, I've managed to avoid injuries so far. My memory, however, seems to be getting worse.

One day I'm standing on the flight deck at another banyan, alone this time, and MS Shelley who is in charge of my Mess storms up to me.

"OS Peffers, you forgot to clean the Mess again!" she tells me angrily.

"I'm so sorry, I'll go do it right away." Feeling terrible, I start to head to the airlock to go below and do the cleaning, but she stops me. "Don't bother, I already did it." With that, she storms off.

Guilt wells up inside me as well as a frustration because I can't fix it. I can't go clean the Mess and make it all good now. I have to just take the heat from the MS.

Again I forget to bring my uniform with me during my workout, and Robertson catches me.

"This is completely unacceptable behaviour in an ordinary seaman, and it's going on your record from now on. Go and get your uniform now, that's an order," he tells me angrily.

"Yes, PO," I say while I walk briskly down the flats with my face turning red. I feel terrible while I go and fetch my uniform from my Mess. Why can't I remember this? Why can't I when others clearly can? Maybe it's the stress of always seeming to be in trouble. Or the poor sleep that I've been having.

The day before we come alongside, the XO comes down to the Cave to give us a talk. He explains that we are on a diplomatic mission and that we all need to act like political representatives of Canada in this port. He tells us that any altercations here could result in an international incident. I had no idea we could be so important.

We're preparing to enter harbour at Busan, and Alders comes to find me in the Cave.

"Hey, Peff, come with me, we're going to man the guardrails. We're entering harbour now."

"Okay, cool," I respond. This is a ritual I learned about in seamanship training.

Alders looks over me critically then, picking a strand of thread from my uniform collar.

"Do you have your ball cap?" she asks.

"I do." I unclip it from the red carabiner on my belt loop and put it on my head.

"You look good," Alders smiles and then leads me up to the fo'c'sle.

Manning the guardrails is a naval tradition. Whenever a military ship enters a friendly port, it's tradition to have the crew display themselves on the upper decks and, historically on sailing vessels, up on the yardarms. The gathering of crew shows that no one is manning the guns.

We climb up to the weather decks and I see majestic rocky cliffs with lush green foliage in the background. The water here is a brilliant turquoise blue. All along the guardrails the ship's company stands equally spaced and at attention. There's a gap on the port bow, and we slip in to complete the chain. I stand at attention proudly. I feel like I'm one with the strength of many. We fly the baby-blue UN flag as we come alongside Busan, South Korea.

BUSAN

The ship is piped secure, and the mass exodus ensues. People don civvies and escape as quickly as possible. While I'm not molly I go on a tour of a Shinto temple. The temple itself is beautiful. My tour group consists of mostly stokers I don't know and a few POs that I also don't know, so no one really talks to me.

I also go off alone and tour downtown Busan including the ultra-modern Starbucks, and only a few blocks away, a traditional fish market. I have lunch in a tiny local noodle shop with no running water or soap in their bathroom. Busan is a mosaic of modern office towers and traditional buildings, often right next to each other. It's stark.

I take a picture of a local Korean lecturing through a megaphone in a busy square and suddenly have to fend off people trying to take my camera away. A PO in my group comes to my defence.

"I'll take that, thank you," the PO says while he snatches my camera from their hands. He hands it to me just as quickly. "Put that away for now, we don't want any trouble," he explains.

"What trouble? What's happening?" I'm confused.

"He's a political protester. He doesn't want his picture taken because the government might find him."

"Oh." That shuts me up. I feel a sudden fear. I guess Koreans aren't as free as Canadians to disagree with their government.

I take a subway where a local woman tries to explain mostly through hand gestures that she's learning English and loves Canada. I show her my pictures on my camera, and she bows deeply to me.

The ship arranges for a tour bus that goes up to the demilitarized zone (DMZ), but unfortunately I'm molly during that time. After the tour is done, LS Gladstone sits in the Cave nursing a beer, trying to explain his experience to me while I wipe down placemats.

"Soldiers staring each other down through the barrels of their guns over a terrain littered with land mines," Gladstone sips from his beer then shakes his head. "It was intense."

"Sounds like it," I say, putting down my cloth for the moment and sitting on the bench opposite him.

"Nothing like it in Canada." More head shaking.

"I guess not, we have it pretty good."

"We are so lucky," Gladstone sips again from his beer. He looks visibly shaken. "It's crazy," he tells me, shaking his head again. "It's just crazy."

No Navy visit to Busan is complete without a visit to Texas Street. There's a direct bus from the ship. Texas Street is a cheap, thronging tourist trap catering to American ships. The guys from the shop take me along, and we end up in a dive of a bar. It's cold here. Indoor heating isn't common, and portable heat lamps are everywhere.

Almost naked, shivering Filipino girls drape themselves over us and beg to be kept warm. The guys love this. Dale has one curled up in his lap. One of the girls pouts and clings to my arm. She rests her head on my shoulder, and before I know what's happening she's pinching playfully at my nipple. The guys really love this. At first I'm suddenly turned on by the attention. My second reaction is to suddenly and painfully realize how lonely I am. I'm confused now. I hide the way I secretly long for more human contact, and carefully I extricate myself.

She settles down, curling up next to me. She whispers in my ear that the owner of the bar keeps her passport so she can't leave, and she's trying to work to save up enough money to bring her sister to live with her here. I am speechless. She looks up at me with beautiful shadowed almond eyes and says maybe it's the same for me. Maybe I'm trapped too.

We stay like this for a while, and I'm relieved, at least for the moment, that the guys are distracted and not scrutinizing me.

On the last day, Jed and I go out for dinner to a local Korean bar-beque. It's delicious and garlic-filled. We stop in at a bar close to Texas Street afterwards and get free shots of vodka from a bunch of Russians.

"They're most likely Russian Mafia," Jed tells me plainly. "Texas Street is basically run by the Russian Mafia."

We walk around drinking bottles of soju openly in public. I get so drunk that I stumble and fall while we make it back to the boat. Jed helps me up while we both laugh.

"Now where did we park that thing…" Jed jokes while we stumble back to the docks.

I notice her up ahead. She's listing. *Winnipeg* sits alone on a jetty, leaning to port quite noticeably. When they designed the CPFs they for-got to take into account the weight of the water in the charged fire main which runs along the port side of the boat. The result is that if the MCR doesn't manually compensate with ballast, the ship lists to port slightly.

At the jetty we both walk independently across the brow. The brow sentry shakes his head and laughs.

MY FIRST WATCH

Someone is gently shaking my shoulder. I open my eyes to dark-red light and JD looking up at me.

"Hey, Peffers," he whispers. "It's 0730, you're on watch in half an hour. Meet Stafford in the MCR at 0740 for rounds."

I reply with a whispered "thanks" and go through my quick morning routine.

Machinery control room (MCR). It's the compartment with all the computer monitors and controls for propulsion, power generation and damage control measures. This room is my official post as an ET. Today is my first day on watch. I finally get to start doing electrical stuff. No more molly. A stoker is the new molly.

Although I don't show it, I'm secretly relieved that I'm no longer molly. I can finally get down to learning my trade, doing the job I signed up for.

By now my morning routine is automatic. I maximize my appearance while minimizing time spent working on my appearance. Today, I only have ten minutes so I make the most of it. I beeline it to the Heads and dunk my head in the sink, quickly washing my face and hair. I quickly towel dry my short blond hair, comb it, and brush my teeth. Next I head to seven Mess and pull on my uniform. I still shower every other day immediately after my sweaty workouts. Getting a shower at 0730 is usually impossible.

Feeling eager, I make my morning commute: about a seventy-metre walk. The MCR is positioned to be in the centre of the ship so it's protected. As I open the door leading to the compartment I notice a brass plaque hanging there. It says, "The prelude to action is the work of the engine room."

I walk in and look around. To my left is the large damage control console. A DC watchkeeper is sitting in front of the console reading a magazine. Along the forward bulkhead is a door leading to the degaussing room, another one of our spaces which houses the controls for the system that neutralizes our magnetic field to protect against WWII-era sea mines which are still a very real threat. In front of the forward bulkhead are two computer terminals that were state of the art in 1990. One belongs to the engineering officer of the watch, who is not an officer at all, but rather a PO 2 stoker who represents the EO. The other belongs to the on-watch stoker. Behind those consoles, in a corner near the aft bulkhead, is my new station, the ET console. The two stokers are reading books. I recognize JD sitting at our console, and he waves me over.

There's a spare chair so I take a seat. JD shows me the controls while we wait for Stafford. There are about a dozen screens that are flipped through by pressing buttons, and a mouse wheel that moves a mouse pointer to select individual pieces of machinery. The screen display is black, and the simple diagrams are displayed in monochrome green.

"Don't worry, you'll get lots of time to get to know the controls," JD tells me.

"Well, this is exciting!" I exclaim. I'm finally in the thick of it, sitting at my console, doing my job.

JD snorts. "You'll get used to it."

An alarm sounds. We both look at the screen and along the bottom in orange text a message appears about HP (high pressure) air limits. I notice no one reacting. Lazily, the on-watch stoker reaches out and presses a button which stops the alarm and goes back to reading. "The alarms are constant; you'll get used to them," JD explains. "They're called nuisance alarms. Slightly miscalibrated instrumentation results in chronic alarms for a lot of the machinery as it cycles on and off."

Another alarm sounds, and another. Both get a quick glance and then they're silenced. There are three kinds of alarm priorities: a low tone, a middle tone, and a high tone alarm. The first one had been a high tone alarm.

"How can people tell when it's a nuisance alarm or when it's a real emergency?" I ask, and JD shrugs his shoulders. "It's just a matter of reading the alarm as it comes in. All you have to do is look at the bottom of the screen."

So basically an imminent explosion will sound the same as something that gets chronically ignored. I cringe internally again.

A low toned alarm comes in, and JD checks his console.

"DG enclosure stage one leak on number two," JD calls over his console to where the engineering officer of the watch is sitting. The engineering officer of the watch swivels around in his chair. "Get the oncoming watchkeeper to drain it," he says.

Stafford shows up then.

"Morning," Stafford says, looking bleary-eyed.

"Evening," says JD. He yawns before continuing. "DG2 needs draining again."

"Okay," Stafford nods, rubbing his eyes.

Stafford shows me how to start rounds then. We start over at the DC console, where a bunch of triangle-shaped metal plaques are hanging. We sign out one in the logbook. He explains to me that it's draped over hatches leading to four or five deck so they are allowed to be open while we check those spaces. Normally *Winnipeg* sails with all her hatches below three deck closed; this slows any floods if they start. The design waterline (DWL) is halfway between three and four deck. Swinging the metal triangle casually, Stafford heads out into the flats.

"It's normal to start rounds all the way aft and head forward," he tells me over his shoulder.

Over the next twenty minutes I'm introduced to a whole new side of *Winnipeg*. We head down into all of her machinery spaces starting with the steering gear compartment. Wherever there is a motor, Stafford shows me how to check its temperature with the back of my hand. There are countless motors. In every compartment we shine our flashlights down into the dark bilges under the catwalks, checking bilge levels. *Winnipeg* is designed to run a dry bilge, but constant leaks fill them instead. We head forward toward her centre and get to her real guts: the four compartments housing propulsion and power generation. From aft to forward they are the aft auxiliary machinery room (AMR), aft engine room (AER), forward engine room (FER), and forward AMR. The AMRs house two generators each, the precious hearts of the ship. They're separated so that if the ship takes damage during combat at one end, then the other end will still have an independent source of power. Diesel generators (DG) three and four are in the aft AMR, DG one and two are in the forward AMR. Stafford explains that DG one is on standby, and DG four is broken. We are running on DGs two and three.

Each generator sits nestled on giant rubber shock absorbent pads and is housed in a noise-reducing acoustic enclosure. The enclosures are grey and are about the size of a minivan. A catwalk weaves its way in between and around them. Along the bulkheads are a dizzying rainbow array of pipes, cables, pumps, motors, monitors, machines, and power panels. The bulkheads are densely packed.

"You'll get to know it all," Stafford tells me. We follow the catwalk that goes around the outside of the generators, and he leans down to touch various motors as he walks.

The AER houses the cruise engine called a propulsion diesel engine (PDE), which we are currently running on. This space is cramped and loud. Stafford leads me along the catwalks, and again I see countless pieces of densely packed machinery and pipes. The FER is the most spacious of engineering spaces and houses our two gas turbines (GTs). I follow as we walk the catwalk around the GT enclosures and take the path leading between them. I'm walking just a few feet away from two engines that are essentially the same as you would find on a Boeing 747. Forty-thousand horsepower sits idle, waiting for action. This space is loud. All the spaces are loud with countless bits of droning machinery. It's a deep booming thrumming sound down here as I walk through the guts of the beast. A few stokers are present, filling in some logs and working.

In the forward AMR, Stafford approaches DG2 droning away happily to itself. He picks a metal rod from its hanging place on the bulkhead and shows me how to insert it at the bottom of the enclosure to turn a valve. I shine my flashlight down at the valve and watch as a stream of greasy black liquid drains into the bilge.

"The DGs are always leaking. They need constant draining," Stafford tells me.

We move on to the fridge flats; I'm already familiar with this place from being molly. Stafford shows me how to log the fridge compressor and then steps into one of the cold rooms to grab himself a yoghurt. We finish our rounds with a trip to the Cave where I gratefully pour myself my first cup of coffee of the day. This time I use a plastic travel mug with *Winnipeg*'s ship logo on it. Stafford fills his mug, and we scarf down a quick breakfast before heading back to the MCR with our coffees in hand.

We return our signed-out metal triangle, and JD does a quick report to Stafford for the changeover. I don't understand any of it. He says, "Two and three, one, two, starboard, starboard, number two." Stafford nods in understanding.

PO 2 Donalds, the oncoming engineering officer of the watch, shows up then. PO 2 Atkins, the current engineering officer of the watch, does a quick report for his replacement. Donalds, now the current engineering officer of the watch, takes over the chair that Atkins just vacated.

"There's a new watchkeeper, OS Peffers, who is double-banked with LS Stafford," PO 2 Atkins tells Donalds.

Donalds looks at me. "You'll be on the same watch as me, so if you ever need anything just come talk to me," he tells me kindly.

JD stands before the engineering officer of the watch, PO 2 Donalds, and says, "Engineering Officer of the Watch, LS Stafford with OS Peffers are your new ET watchkeepers."

The engineering officer of the watch looks up from his console and says, "Very good," and with that JD bids us goodnight and leaves the MCR. Stafford sits at his console for a few minutes, flipping through the various pages.

"Just to see if anything has changed since we last looked," he tells me.

And things are always changing. There are always multiples of machinery which rotate on and off. I keep track of which generators are running, which engines we're using, which lube oil pumps are on, the running fire main pump, which steering pump is on, and much more. I will know her from the inside now.

When we're on watch we're expected to do maintenance. If an engineering emergency or bong-bongs occur, then we get back to our station in the MCR. For the rest of the watch, Stafford shows me how to do lamp-ups. That's the Navy's fancy term for changing light bulbs. He assures me I'll be doing a lot of these. It's a simple procedure, and after a few examples I have it down. We walk through the ship with armfuls of fluorescent lights and a stepladder, following the defect list. I reach up and unfasten the light cover, twist out the burnt-out tube, and twist in its replacement. As reward, sudden bright light greets me as the new tube lights up. I smile to myself because I'm finally doing it; I'm starting to fix her.

THE WATCHES

As I settle into the watch rotation, my circadian rhythm is destroyed. I'm up at all hours of the day and night. I'm sitting in the chart room with Jed one morning just after I started being on watch.

"So you're on the watches now," Jed observes.

"Yeah, finally."

"How do you like it compared to being molly?"

"Well, I'm getting less sleep, so I'm more tired, but I'm not cleaning anymore. I guess it has its pros and cons," I pause before I continue. "Do you ever stand watches?"

"I used to, back when I was a corporal. Man, did they suck ass!" Jed leans back in his chair. "Now I'm a cushy day worker like most of the senior staff on-board," Jed turns his back briefly to his computer and rummages in a filing cabinet behind his desk. He pulls out a bag of chocolate-covered coffee beans and offers me the bag.

"Oh, thanks." Gratefully, I take a handful. I can use all the stimulation I can get, and that includes chocolate-covered coffee beans.

"The watch system is an antiquated, low-grade torture device first invented by Nelson's Navy," Jed says, popping a few beans into his mouth. "Designed to keep the crew at a low-grade level of exhaustion so they aren't inclined to mutiny."

"Really?" My heart sinks a little.

"Solid naval tradition has simply kept it in place all these years." Jed takes a last handful of coffee beans and puts the bag back in his filing cabinet.

The twenty-four-hour period is broken up into four-hour watches. My schedule breaks down as follows and simply repeats itself every four days:

Day One:

Morning: 0400 to 0800 (4 a.m. to 8 a.m.)

Turning-To: 0800 to 1600 (8 a.m. to 4 p.m.)

Second Dogs: 1800 to 2000 (6 p.m. to 8 p.m.)

Day Two:

Forenoon: 0800 to 1200 (8 a.m. to 12 p.m.)

Turning-To: 1200 to 1600 (12 p.m. to 4 p.m.)

Firsts: 2000 to 0000 (8 p.m. to 12 a.m.)

Day Three:

Turning-To: 0800 to 1200 (8 a.m. to 12 p.m.)

Afternoon: 1200 to 1600 (12 p.m. to 4 p.m.)

Mids: 0000 to 0400 (12 a.m. to 4 a.m.)

Day Four:

Turning-To: 1200 to 1600 (12 p.m. to 4 p.m.)

First Dogs: 1600 to 1800 (4 p.m. to 6 p.m.)

Morning: 0400 to 0800 (4 a.m. to 8 a.m.)

The Engineering Div stands one-in-three and one-in-four watches, meaning one in every three or four watches you are on watch, then you skip three or four watches and are on watch again. If you are one-in-four like I am, then whenever you aren't on watch and the time of day is between 0800 and 1600 you are Turning-To, meaning you are working.

It's a small mercy that after doing the Mids you are permitted to turn-to at noon instead of 0800. Days where we have more than six hours off in the evenings are called super-all-nighters and are like mini weekends where most of the ship's company socializes in the Cave around their two beers. Most of the ship's company aren't as crazy busy as me.

Because of my gruelling training schedule, when I'm not on watch or Turning-To I'm working on my training packages. I have little time for things like socializing or sleeping.

When I'm on watch and all the lamp-ups have been done, I'm required to sit in a corner of the MCR studying my packages, drawing my electrical diagrams and reading the technical manuals. No one talks to me, and I don't talk to anyone. A strange kind of isolation begins to surround me. All around me, the other watchkeepers chat and laugh with each other or read books and magazines. I'm the only one doing a training package on my watch, so I'm the only one sitting alone in the corner. I start to really miss human connection.

Every few days I find ten or fifteen minutes to go up to the bridge. I lean tiredly against my hard steel pole. I see so little daylight now that when I go above decks I squint painfully in the bright sunlight. The OOW tells me we're en route to Singapore. On the way back down into the ship again I stop in at the chart room to visit Jed. He's always happy to see me, though he sees less of me now. He lets me in on what's happening on the ship.

"The plan is to only stop for a few hours in Singapore to get fitted with a new weapon," he tells me.

"Oh really? What kind of weapon?" I ask from the chart table.

"An LRAD, long-range acoustic device," Jed says. "It uses sound waves to cause debilitating pain and nausea on its targets," he explains plainly. "It's a new kind of non-lethal weapon that NATO is trying out."

"So, we're getting ready for combat?"

"The rumours about the anti-piracy mission are looking more and more to be true," Jed says carefully. "Nothing official yet, you know how it is."

"Don't believe it until it's actually happening," I say pedantically. The military is known for changing plans at the last minute.

"The plan is to sail with our new weapon out of Singapore," Jed says, "then to the coast of Somalia. Then we enter the Box in the Gulf of Aden."

"The Box, that's our area of responsibility under NATO, right?"

"Our own little square of ocean," Jed acknowledges.

"That should be exciting."

"It'll be mostly boredom," Jed explains. "We circle our Box over and over and for the most part don't do much."

"Well, at least we're participating," I say, trying for optimism.

"We might get lucky and catch a pirate," Jed says hopefully.

As we head further and further south the ocean temperature gradually rises. *Winnipeg's* hull below the waterline starts to heat up. All the spaces on three deck upward are cooled by air conditioning. As the engineering spaces heat up, people doing rounds and work down there start to sweat. To compensate, boxes of Camelbak drinking water packs are brought out of storage. The boxes are simply left in the Cave, and it's a free-for-all. By the time I hear about them they're all gone. They mostly went to stokers who spend a lot of on-watch time hanging out in the Cave.

The rest of the ETOWs are doing one-in-three watches, which means I have a different ETOW for all my watches. Everyone I work with seems to have a different approach to training me, and they all want me to learn different things. Robertson explains this approach during one of his cramped shop meetings, "You'll get maximum exposure to the learning process by getting everyone's approach."

But the result is mostly confusion and forgetfulness on my part.

"You'll get it, Peff," LS Pellier says kindly.

"Yeah, just need time and experience," Kelvin says.

"Here, this might help as a training aid," Robertson digs in his uniform jacket pocket and produces a small notepad. He hands it over to me.

"Thanks, PO," I say, stashing it in my pants pocket. Now whenever someone starts to tell me about a system, I take it out and start taking notes which I can refer to later.

PO 2 Mann, my Training PO, reviews my training progress and tells me I'm keeping a good pace. I'm done my seamanship training package now, and the Deck Department signs it off and puts me on the list for alongside DC watchkeeping. Technically, in order to be a DC watchkeeper I need to take a course at the DC school. The ship is so short on DC watchkeepers that this rule is ignored. One day while heading into the MCR I take a look at the DC console. It's huge and intimidating with hundreds of buttons and indicating lights. I'm not looking forward to my first DC watch.

A steady stream of lamp-ups continue with my watches. On watch with Pellier, he pulls out a neat device. It's a plastic hand-held sensor

that lights up red and beeps in the presence of the magnetic field associ-
ated with electricity. He uses it while we're troubleshooting the burnt-
out lights.

"It reminds me of something out of *Star Trek*," Pellier says while
waving it near a cable.

Occasionally the ETOW will be called to a specific compartment
on ship to troubleshoot something that needs to be repaired right away.
When this happens with Pellier, he hands me the ETOW tool bag and
I follow him. When we show up to look at the piece of machinery, he
jokingly says, "Please state the nature of the electrical emergency."

One day while doing a lamp-up in the aft air conditioning (AC)
plant, I neglect to dog the door open properly and the ship rolls. The
door slams shut. Because of the change in air pressure inside versus outside the AC plant, a strong suction develops which holds the door closed.
In order for someone of my size to wrench the door open I have to brace
one foot on the bulkhead next to the door and pull with all my strength.
There isn't enough space inside the compartment for me to do that, so I
can't open the door. I'm trapped.

I think for a moment about how to escape. Pressing a few buttons
on the controller, I shut down the AC. After a few minutes the suction is
reduced, and I can open the door again. I head back to the MCR where
Alders is sitting at the DC console with a book.

"Hi, Leading Seaman," I say.

"Hey, Peff."

"I had to shut down the aft AC plant. I put it in local then turned
it off for a few minutes."

"Oh, that was you," Alders swivels in her chair to look at a flashing
indicating light on the DC console.

"Yeah, the door slammed shut and the suction had me trapped."

"That's a relief," Alders laughs a little, pressing a button on the console. The flashing light stops flashing. "I thought that something else had
just broken around here," Alders continues, going back to her book. "The
defect list is long enough."

Nobody wants to replace ballasts. Mounted above the fluorescent
tubes, they are the white metal boxes that control the flow of current
going to the lights. Over the years the housings for the ballasts have

been bent out of shape from not completely unscrewing the attachments. As a result it's usually a wrestling match to jam a replacement ballast in place. All the ETOWs skip over the ballasts, and they are left for me to do. One time I spend a good ten or fifteen minutes bending bits of metal and forcing things into place, and I start to feel frustrated. I swear loudly and hit the thing with the handle of my screwdriver, finally wedging it in place. As luck would have it, the coxn happens to be walking by. He pauses to give me a warning look before he walks on.

A few days later I'm called to the shop while I'm Turning-To. Robertson and Alders are waiting for me with serious looks on their faces. The door is closed, and I am trapped.

"OS Peffers, you've been observed working unsafely while doing lamp-ups," Alders explains in a stern tone of voice. "You need to wear safety glasses."

Nobody in the ET shop wears safety glasses. I don't even know where to find a pair. The closest thing to safety glasses are the RAS goggles attached to the RAS hard hat.

"The closest thing to safety glasses around here is the RAS goggles…" I start to say.

But Robertson pipes up, "OS Peffers, you are talking back again and that is completely unacceptable. This incident is going on your file."

More frustration starts to well up inside me.

"Sorry, PO." I try to keep my voice as even as possible.

"Look around the shop, check the drawers, I'm sure we have safety glasses," Robertson says impatiently.

"And you really need to stop talking back, OS Peffers," Alders says.

"Yes, Leading Seaman," I say while inside my frustration blends with guilt. No one else is being told to wear safety glasses. I keep screwing up so I keep getting noticed, so I keep being singled out.

One day while working out in the reserve space doing some weight training I happen to be working out at the same time as the doc.

"How is your finger doing?" WO Lyall asks me while adding a plate to the bench-press machine.

"Oh, fine," I say, picking up some free weights and preparing for some biceps curls.

"You know, you have great muscle tone."

I smile and blush slightly at the compliment. "Oh, thanks."

"I mean it, you've probably got more muscle tone than most men on-board."

"You think so?"

"You could really work it up though, with the right tips and adjustments to your form."

I'm about to start the biceps curls, but now I pause. "Adjustments?"

"Yeah, the best way to get the hardest workout for your biceps is to do the reps sitting at an angle and letting your arms hang down to start. Here, take a seat." The doc pulls the bench back up to an eighty-degree incline and motions with his hands for me to sit down.

"Oh, thank you," I say while I place myself on the bench. Weights are in each hand, my arms falling slightly backward. I feel the stretch across my chest.

"Okay, now do your arm curl."

I bring the weights up toward my shoulders, feeling my biceps flex. I repeat the motion, and the familiar ache of a tiring muscle returns during the reps, but sooner than normal for me.

"Wow, I can really feel that."

"Feel it? That's your bicep getting bigger." The doc pauses with his arms across his chest. "You have amazing biceps definition."

"Oh, thank you," I say. He waits for me to do my sets, then he continues with his tutoring, showing me how to maximize stretching and strengthening my body. I spend a good hour with him tutoring me on my form at weight training.

Speaking of tutoring, we start doing regular RASs every five days or so. I'm driven from my precious rack outside of my on watch and Turning-To schedule to spend a few hours as RAS ET. If we RAS while I'm on watch, someone covers for my watch.

The refuelling process involves sailing at about a twenty metre distance away from the fuelling ship and matching speed. The RAS buffer (usually a PO 2 bosun) fires the RAS gun toward the other ship, or the other ship fires at us. The RAS gun launches a large rubber bullet attached to a nylon string. If they fire on us, we take shelter behind bulkheads or deck equipment. The string attached to the RAS gun is tied to a larger line, which is hauled across to the other ship, which gets attached to the spanwire, which is hauled across and clipped into place. The spanwire then sends across a line attached to a set of hoses. The line is given three turns around the capstan, which is when my work begins.

I stand with the controller to the capstan in my hands and follow the orders of the RAS buffer to heave in handsomely (which means at low speed) or roundly (which means at high speed). The turning capstan causes the hose to be drawn across under electric power. The hoses weigh hundreds of pounds. The hose connects to a bell in the side of the ship, and once the hose is seated my job is done. I still have to stand around with the controls in my hands in case there are any emergencies for the few hours it takes to pump over enough fuel to fill our tanks. While we wait a large bucket of candy is passed around; this is called RAS candy.

It's a tradition to send across gifts from our ship when the hoses get returned, and the fuelling ship sends across gifts to us when they send their hoses over. We usually send a plastic-wrapped package with our ship's ball cap and crest. The fuelling ship usually sends over a bottle of scotch and some stickers. The scotch and stickers never make it to junior ranks.

Once we are done receiving fuel, the breakaway tradition is followed. Either ship plays a breakaway song through their upper deck speakers. The song is arranged in advance and usually has a break-up theme. This time the fuelling ship plays Stealers Wheel's "Stuck In the Middle With You." They are fuelling another ship on their port side while they fuel us on their starboard side. There are smiles and laughs all around.

DRILLS

Engineering drills become part of my daily life now. Everyday during the afternoon, the EO comes down to the MCR and holds a meeting with all the watchkeepers. The EO presses his closed palm into the palm of his open hand to emphasize his words.

"Engineering drills are important, we never know what's going to break. That's why it's important to carry out these drills daily, it's just Basic." He looks us all in the eyes. "We need to be well-prepared for the event of an engineering emergency." His handsome face looks concerned, "These drills are important."

PO 2 Mann starts a special computer program which runs a simulated ship on the consoles in the MCR. High-pitched alarms come in that are serious, like the loss of a fuel pump, an overheating bearing, or a tripped engine. These are just simulated though. Orders are issued by the engineering officer of the watch; the EO simply observes from a managerial position. Stoker roundsmen are dispatched quickly, and they practice getting to the piece of equipment and using the shincom to call back to the MCR with simulated damage info.

I mostly just stand around for these drills, but occasionally I get called to monitor bearing temperatures down in the FER. In the event of a motor failing, I get to go and investigate. It's fun to pretend there's an emergency. I get to walk quickly through the flats with my tool bag slung over my shoulder. People see me coming and move out of my way. PO 2 Perrant stands by the affected piece of equipment to supervise, and I get to open up the controller and use my multimeter and occasionally pull a simulated blown fuse.

The drills tend to be repetitive though. It's the same half-dozen simulations that repeat themselves. The most common drill is a steering gear breakdown. As soon as the alarm comes in, I have to grab my bag and head aft at a fast walk all the way to the steering gear compartment. Robertson is waiting for me with a clipboard in hand. I practise pressing the required buttons on the controller and taking the wheel which connects directly to the rudder post. The bosunmate arrives from the bridge out of breath and gets on comms with the OOW to continue steering manually. It's my job to turn the wheel as the bosunmate gives me the steering directions. Robertson gets to debrief us afterwards in the flats outside the steering gear compartment, and even if I do everything perfectly he'll always tell me I need to be faster.

One day the hydraulic pipes that move the rudder post start jumping out at me. Instead of a smooth application of force, the lines pulse intermittently. One of the metal pipes almost hits me in the face while I lean over them to steer by solenoids. I briefly wonder about the pressure inside those pipes and the probable injury that would result if they broke. The compartment is filled with people of all ranks though, and I suddenly realize I trust them now with my life.

Once the drill is stopped, everyone is called back to the MCR and the EO debriefs us. At first I'm screwing up every drill, forgetting what I need to do. The EO makes sure he tells me to get better at my job. When the EO gives me feedback it's different though. He has a constant air of respect about him; when he tells me I need to improve it's not in a condescending, judgmental tone of voice but rather a gentle almost imploring tone of voice. I want to get better just to please him.

It's not long before I'm harbouring a secret crush on the EO. He's quite attractive physically, and I like his personality. The stokers jokingly call him rabbit-face because they claim he has a face like a rabbit. A plastic rabbit lawn ornament has been placed on top of the stokers' console in honour of the EO.

One day during drills *Winnipeg*'s low-pressure air system fails and the high-pressure air system has to be diverted into a reducing station to feed the low-pressure air supply. Low-pressure air is used to power the pneumatic valves throughout the engineering spaces. An unexpected high-pitched alarm comes in on the last remaining console that monitors the real *Winnipeg*.

The on-watch stoker calls out, "There's an HP air leak at the cross-connect valve!"

All joking in the background stops. The drill stops. The engineering officer of the watch orders a series of valves to be closed. The roundsmen are recalled, and they quickly file into the MCR. The on-watch stoker's fingers fly over the controls.

The leak is quickly isolated, and a repair team is assembled to go down and fix it. A few hours later the repair job is done, and I'm sitting in the corner at my table, now off watch, but working on my training package.

I listen in while the engineering officer of the watch reports to the chief ERA that the leak has been sealed. A faulty rubber O-ring is to blame. The rubber had deteriorated with age and simply broke when the valve was turned. The engineering officer of the watch then asks the chief ERA if they should check the rest of the O-rings in the system; they are all the same age.

The chief ERA pauses to consider it then tells him, "Don't bother."

Don't bother? A ring main of small-gauge, high-pressure lines runs through all four engineering spaces. There's no avoiding the ring main as it runs along the deckhead. You have to pass it while you go up or down the ladder into the space. When I'm doing rounds I'm required to get cozy with the compressor to read the gauges on these lines when logging it. If one O-ring just gave out, how many more are ready to give out? It was pure luck that no one was in the space when the leak occurred. In just a few hours I have to go down there again.

I'm doing rounds with Stafford, who keeps emphasizing memorization of all the power panel locations in the engineering spaces. I automatically pull out my pad of paper and start writing. By now I'm sucking back coffee the way *Winnipeg*'s GTs suck back fuel. I'm starting to notice a definite decline in my ability to memorize things, though I try hard. It's the sleep deprivation.

Stafford approaches one of the HP air lines and jumps up, grabbing it with his hands. He does a few chin-ups on the line while I cringe. He laughs.

I'm on watch for the Mids, and the ship is bathed in dark-red night light. The flats are empty of people, and I can get some space. Kelvin has just shown me how to clean the slip rings on the shaft grounding system.

PO 2 Donalds calls me over to his console and tells me to go down into the AER and clean the slip rings on the shaft there. I comply with a "Yes, PO" and grab the cleaning stick from behind the ETOW chair. Before I leave, Donalds briefs me on safety procedures in the event that the hydraulic start pack for the GT starts when I'm in the space. He tells me that the line pressure gets so high that if I'm next to it and a line breaks I would be seriously injured, so to take cover by stepping behind the PDE enclosure. The hydraulic start packs are used to start the GTs.

I head down the ladder into the AER alone this time. I eye the HP air lines suspiciously as I pass beneath them. A sudden loud hissing noise erupts from the space and I jump, heart pounding. It's just the low-pressure air compressor cycling. The stokers tell me everyone starts out jumpy but that I'll get used to all the sudden loud noises. I stand on the catwalk and notice that I'm quite alone down here. All of *Winnipeg's* pounding, thrumming insides full of tightly contained energy seem to press in on me. I shrug the feeling off and get to work. I start cleaning the slip rings as ordered.

After a few minutes I hear the hydraulic start pack begin to start up. It starts with a low-pitched loud humming noise that gradually increases in pitch as the pressure builds up. I pull my stick back from the shaft and I take cover behind the PDE enclosure like I was told. Before the start pack can go through its complete cycle it falls silent again. I think this is a bit weird, but I get back and continue with my job.

Again the start pack begins its cycle and again I go behind the PDE enclosure for cover. It stops again suddenly in mid-cycle. I get back and continue cleaning and again it starts up. I can't get my job done like this so now I just duck down behind the shaft. Again it stops early. I stand up and begin to work again. This cycle of the hydraulic start pack starting and stopping after I duck continues for several minutes. I'm getting quite distressed for the safety of the hydraulic start pack at this point. I don't know what the added stress of quickly starting and stopping is doing to it. It's not designed to run like this. Maybe it's breaking right now; I start to have horrible images of high-pressure explosions blowing my limbs off. Nothing to do but bleed out all alone in agony for my last few seconds.

I start to feel the urge to run out of the space. I try to keep working, but eventually the start pack is starting and stopping so rapidly it's cycling on and off once a second. I'm ducking below the shaft and then it dawns on me. Donalds is probably operating the start pack from the MCR and is watching me through the CCTV camera mounted on the opposite bulkhead. He probably thinks this is funny. I'm distressed now because I can't do my job as ordered. I'm not going to stay standing out in the open while it starts up, not after that safety brief.

I can't take it anymore, and with my heart pounding and the start pack starting and stopping rapidly I quickly run up the ladder and out into the relative safety of three deck.

I head back to the MCR, and Donalds and a few stokers are huddled around Donalds's console laughing. "I can't do my job safely while you're operating the start pack like that," I tell Donalds bluntly.

"Don't talk to me in that tone of voice, Ordinary Seaman! As engineering officer of the watch I can run the GT water washes whenever I like," he replies angrily. GT water washes are usually done at night and involve using the start pack just once to start the GT.

My stress increases even more: Robertson assigns more work for me. Now I have my training packages to complete, the cathodics reports to do, I'm the RAS ET, and it's my responsibility to ensure all the uninterruptible power supply (UPS) filters are cleaned. The only other person in the shop with secondary duties is Stafford; he manages the electrical stores. Everybody else just gets to show up for their watches and hang out.

We have tons of uninterruptible power supplies scattered throughout the ship in all kinds of random places. They are about the size of a bar fridge and provide fifteen minutes of battery power to essential systems in the event of a blackout. They have a filter screwed to the air intake on their fronts; these filters require periodic removal and cleaning. Each unit has one filter, and they all need to be cleaned once every thirty days. Most of the UPSs are found in *Winnipeg*'s engineering spaces. I get even less sleep now.

I'm climbing all over machinery down in the machinery spaces to get at various out-of-the-way UPSs. One of the devices is bolted to the deckhead which is two storeys up from the catwalk. I keep thinking about the high-pressure air lines and the hydraulic start packs. I no longer feel safe down here when I'm alone. I don't know what else might break or blow up at any moment.

I'm down in the forward AMR collecting filters, and I see a stoker doing maintenance on one of the desalinators. He sees me and waves then goes back to his work. I relax, feeling safe again. I'm okay with dying slowly with my limbs torn off so long as someone could be there with me for my last moments.

I'm in the FER all alone. There are half a dozen UPSs located in an area of the space called LOSCA. The acronym has something to do with lube oil storage. Feeling the fear, I step gingerly past the silent hydraulic start pack which might start up at any moment and get to where I can access LOSCA, which is between the two giant gear boxes right in front of the GTs. I climb up a ladder and now I'm trapped on top of the GTs. There's no quick emergency escape hatch in LOSCA. I work quickly, removing the filters, bagging them as fast as I can.

Then it happens: I hear the hydraulic start pack begin to spool up. One of the GTs that I'm standing practically on top off is about to start. I freeze, crouching down on the catwalk and wait for oblivion as the start pack reaches its high-pitched end cycle. The starboard GT fires to life behind me, and I turn to face it. It sounds like a raging inferno inside its enclosure, and LOSCA begins to vibrate. Is that a normal sound? I've never been down in the FER with a GT running before. My anxiety peaks, and I drop my bag. I practically jump down from LOSCA, run through a quick maze of pipes, dodging motors here and there and emerge at the base of the ladder leading out of the space. Before I know it I'm standing in the airlock, breathing hard, heart pounding.

I take a minute to calm down then I force myself back down the ladder and along the catwalk and up the ladder again to LOSCA to retrieve my bag of filters. A deep shame starts to fill me because I can't seem to shake the fear when I'm down there alone.

One day Alders comes into the MCR while I'm on watch.

"OS Peffers, after your watch, come find me in the shop," she says, her tone all business.

"Yes, Leading Seaman." My chest squeezes with anxiety. I get the sense that I'm in trouble again and wonder what it's about.

I get to the shop after my watch is done.

"Follow me. We're going to visit your Div O," Alders says before leaving the shop. I follow behind her. "It's time for your PDR," she says over her shoulder.

She escorts me up to two deck to my Div O's cabin. PDR stands for personnel development report. I sit on his couch with Alders while he sits at his desk and I am made to read over my PDR.

The block of text says that I am progressing in a timely fashion with my training but I lack the correct attitude to be successful in the Navy. I need to accept criticism and feedback from superiors. My immediate reaction is to criticize my PDR, which I realize would just serve to illustrate my inability to accept criticism. Instead I simply sign to say that I have read and understood my PDR, and when my Div O asks me if I have any questions I give him a curt "No, sir."

I'm in the shop one day at the computer, filling in the cathodics report. Pellier walks into the shop and chats for a bit.

"Hey, Peff, how's it going?" He leans against the opposite counter.

"Fine," I shrug while I continue to type.

"Hey, you know, Alders is taking daily div notes on you. Did you know that?" Pellier's tone is gentle.

"Daily? No, I didn't know that." Again I feel the anxiety of being in trouble again.

"What did you do to piss her off?"

"Alders? I don't know." I try to focus on my data entry task to stay calm.

"She's probably under orders from the PO 1," Pellier says thoughtfully. "What did you do to piss him off? That's the real question."

I feel trapped as I sit at the computer, continuing my cathodics report.

I'm meeting JD in the MCR at 0340 for rounds before the Morning watch. The Morning watch is the worst watch to get up for. I'm barely awake when he meets me and starts to lead me aft for rounds.

As we climb down ladders again I start to wake up from the exercise. When we get to the machinery spaces, he says, "PO 1 Robertson wants me to give you a complete set of rounds today."

And with that he pulls an iPod from his jacket pocket, puts the ear buds in his ears and takes me down into the spaces.

It's the middle of the night, so we are the only people in the space. Normally MP3 players are not permitted except during workouts or while taking breaks while off watch. He leads me up a series of ladders in the aft AMR that I hadn't even noticed were there until now. We climb up and up until we are at a catwalk probably four storeys above where we started down in five deck. Up here there are only a few fluorescent lights so it's quite dark. As we climb it gets hotter too. At the catwalk JD takes the ladder that's against the bulkhead here and starts to climb up again. I look down briefly through the grating of the catwalk and see a long way to fall, four storeys down to hard unforgiving machinery parts. The ship continues to sway rhythmically all the while as I follow JD up the new ladder.

We climb up another two storeys until we get to a deckhead with a particularly dirty looking hatch in it. It's dark, hot, and high up. I wait on the ladder while JD pulls his uniform jacket sleeves over his hands then puts his covered hands on the wheel above his head. He turns the wheel, and the hatch pops open. I see pure blackness through the opening. JD swings the hatch fully open and climbs up, coming to stand on the deck waiting for me. I climb up through the hatch into an even hotter darker part of the ship. I stand on the deck and look about.

"The hatch wheel is too hot to touch with bare skin," JD explains.

I'm in a small compartment one storey high with a dirty red emergency escape hatch in the deckhead. The walls are completely black, and there is only one working fluorescent light in the space. It's dark and hot. Just a few feet away is the exhaust from the engines and generators. There's a deep boiling sound coming from the bulkhead where exhaust is escaping from the ship. We are in the farthest reaches of *Winnipeg*, at the top of the inside of the exhaust stack.

"This part of the ship is so dirty it's simply painted black," JD tells me while he glances around.

I nod and look around in silence.

JD continues, "This compartment is called the Black Deck. Nobody comes up here unless they absolutely have to."

A NEW WEAPON

I'm so busy with my work both on watch and off that I don't even notice when we come alongside in Singapore. There is no time for me to sit at the ET table in the Cave and socialize while I eat anymore. This adds another layer of isolation to my new existence. I'm walking into the Cave one day to grab a snack because I worked through mealtime, and suddenly there's a stranger standing in the Cave wearing plain work overalls. I stop short, disoriented and a little shocked. By now I've gotten to know the face of every person on-board, and they wear the same blue and black uniform.

I stop and stare at this strange new person, and I can't resolve my confusion. I feel like someone has just invaded my personal space. How did they get on-board? Who are they? Then it dawns on me that *Winnipeg* has gone very still, and I figure we must be alongside now. It turns out we are offering to feed the dockworkers who are doing work on our boat, and this is a dockworker from Singapore.

Because we are only staying for a few hours, the regular watch rotation is kept. Today is just like any other sailing day. I get a few minutes of free time during the day, and I head up and out the airlock. The air is thick with humidity here, so much so that the lens of my camera steams up instantly. Dockworkers wave happily to me from the jetty.

We have lost our primary masthead steaming light and are running on the secondary. While the ship is stationary the ETs go to work fixing the light. Stafford dons a three-point harness and scales the mast. He unfastens the fixture and brings it down to the shop for inspection and repair. The plastic housing is waterlogged and crusted with salt. After it's cleaned and the bulb is replaced, Alders lets me seal up the plastic housing with a bright-blue silicone gel. I have a moment of pleasure in the shop while I get to work with my hands and listen to music.

A few days ago for comic relief, Kelvin was playing around with some grease and applied it to his face under his eyes like a hockey player. Everyone had a good laugh. Thinking of this I apply some of the blue gel to my face. Alders comes into the shop briefly and tells me, "OS Peffers, that gel is a skin irritant; you should probably go wash it off."

"Okay, Leading Seaman," I say absently while I work. I continue to work and figure since it's not burning me I'll wash it off once I'm done. Alders comes back into the shop.

"OS Peffers, I've already told you to go wash your face, and you haven't followed my orders. This incident will be noted. Go and immediately wash your face right now," Alders says in a stern voice, then she leaves the shop.

As soon as she's gone I hear a pipe for storing ship. All junior ranks are expected to help with this, and I will be in trouble if any POs catch me not storing ship. I face a sudden crisis. If I follow Alders's orders and go to the Heads to wash my face, I risk being found as not helping with storing ship. If I store ship like the pipe has ordered me to do and wait to wash my face, then I risk getting in even more trouble with Alders. Isn't this ridiculous?

I spend a minute debating my fate, then I quickly make my way to the Heads to wash my face first. I don't want any more trouble with Alders. I've just finished wiping my face clean in front of the mirror in the female Heads when a female master seaman enters and tells me, "You're supposed to be storing ship, not admiring your appearance in the mirror!"

"I was ordered to…"

"You have a real reputation for talking back, and this incident will be reported to your chain of command," she tells me angrily, "OS Peffers, you are to report immediately for storing ship."

A stab of irritation flashes through me as I make my way out of the Heads. With all these little incidents occurring I no longer feel sorry or guilty, but angry instead.

That evening I go up to the bridge as we are exiting harbour. The sun is setting and the sky is a beautiful rainbow of pastel colours. The ocean reflects the sky beautifully. We're in a large harbour in a long line of ships waiting our turn to exit. I see numerous large tankers hanging on the horizon in front of us. Behind us is the modern skyline of Singapore lit up and looking beautiful. Jed comes to stand next to me on the bridge and we watch together as we slowly make our way out to sea again.

Standing together with Jed in an easy silence, I feel comforted by his presence. It's a stark contrast to how I feel around my shop.

CROSSING THE LINE

We're all set to cross the equator. The ship has been preparing for days. Now we coast idly in warm tropical waters. The day starts with a special pipe from Davy Jones done in a Scottish brogue by one of the combat chiefs. He calls all tadpoles to dine at their special crossing-the-line breakfast. Watches are forgotten for today, which is a special Navy day. Essential systems are being monitored by a skeleton crew.

Since this is my first time crossing the equator, I'm a tadpole. Once you have crossed it you become a shellback forevermore. Most of the ship's company are tadpoles, and a small crusty selection of chiefs and POs are shellbacks. The whole day is designed to be one big hazing ritual.

We are herded into the Cave, and our plates are filled with food-colouring-soaked bacon and eggs and hash browns. They have names like mermaid's ovaries and sea monster tongue. The food colouring wouldn't be so bad except the cooks have added flavourings to the food. The doc has inspected it all and given it the medical go ahead. None of it is technically poisonous.

The hash browns are soaked in pickle juice and something sweet that completely grates with the briny pickle flavour. It's disgusting. At every table, the blue cleaning buckets have been laid out. What are the buckets for, you might ask?

Right next to me, an OS grabs the bucket and leans over, vomiting into it. As soon as he's done, someone across from me starts gagging and grabs for the bucket. I sit with my food, determined to get through this ordeal as quickly as possible. Chew chew swallow. I try not to taste as I swallow it down. A particularly chewy piece of bacon fat that's been marinating in vinegar graces my tongue, and I gag. I swallow it down quickly and shudder, taking another bite and another.

All around the Cave are the sounds of people gagging and retching or complaining. A few PO shellbacks supervise the meal and laugh, telling us to eat up. In order for us to leave the room our plates have to be empty. It doesn't matter how much of it you keep down, you just have to eat it all once. The food is cold, slimy, and gross. I quickly learn that I can't gag and swallow at the same time. I work away at my plate with single-minded determination to just swallow it all as quickly as possible.

I see MS Hampton at another table having a horrible time with his breakfast. He takes a bite then vomits into a bucket. He takes another bite and vomits again. I'm almost done now. I haven't vomited once. A shiver runs down my spine as another piece of soaking bacon fat enters my mouth.

Victory! Huzzah, my plate is empty. I sit for a moment contemplating how my stomach feels and decide I'll be fine. Heartburn is already welling up painfully in my chest. I'm one of the last tadpoles to leave the Cave, and I see a few stragglers looking green in the face. One of them gags but doesn't grab the bucket in time and vomits the food back onto his plate. The shellback PO nearest him laughs and slaps him on the back, leaning in close to watch him eat everything on his plate.

The rest of the day is spent playing a kind of cat and mouse game between the tadpoles and the shellbacks. The shellbacks have taken over the chief's and PO's Mess while the tadpoles are defending the Cave. People travel in groups for protection. Groups of marauding shellbacks invade and capture tadpoles. I'm grabbed suddenly while a group of us tadpoles attempt to make it up to the fo'c'sle.

An old chief has my arms in a vice grip and I play struggle at first, but then I realize he really is trapping me. I struggle with all my might and he's still stronger than me. Surrendering, I'm not sure how to feel. He drags me off to the chief's and PO's Mess where he ties me to one of the plush arm chairs.

I haven't seen the chief's and PO's Mess before, and I marvel at the modern bleached oak wood paneling and how much nicer their tables and chairs are compared to the Cave. The class system is alive and well in the Navy. The junior NCMs are the lower class, the chiefs and POs are the middle class, and the officers, who are served only by stewards, are the upper class.

It's not long before the tadpoles launch an attack on the chief's and PO's Mess. We have our numbers in our favour, and someone quickly unties me. I get back to the Cave and find that a few other ODs have been tied up to the love seats while the Cave was empty.

In the afternoon the ship's company is piped up to the flight deck, and everyone assembles for the ritual that's to follow. Fat men wearing coconuts for breasts and wigs and tight-fitting, mermaid-style skirts sit on the edge of a large hot tub that the hull techs have thrown together. Inside it is a soupy mixture of mustard and water. Behind the mermaids and the hot tub is King Neptune's Court. I see Jed, wearing a white doctor's coat and stethoscope, standing with a large jar in front of him. The CO and XO are both there dressed like lizards donning tridents.

One by one the tadpoles come forward and in front of the entire ship's company have to do three things. First, there's a pan brought before them with a rotting fish in it. They have to kiss the fish. Next, they step up to the doctor, and Jed feeds them their pills. The pills are maraschino cherries soaked in way too much hot sauce. Depending on how large the crowd's cheer is, Jed feeds them between one and three pills. Lots of people gag as they try to chew and swallow. Last, they have to get dunked in the hot tub so that the stinging briny water covers their head at least once. I watch and laugh while people go through these three steps. Once they're dunked, King Neptune's Court yells "Clean!" and the former tadpoles become shellbacks.

I watch Alders go through her hazing and just before they dunk her, the lizard CO and XO suddenly produce master seaman epaulettes and begin replacing her leading seaman epaulettes while standing on either side of her. She's being promoted. The crowd cheers. Alders smiles one of her charming, perfect smiles.

I clap with the crowd, feeling a stab of jealousy at her good image, but still happy for her promotion.

When it's my turn to go up, I kiss the rotting, stinking fish while holding my breath. Next Jed stands before me and according to the cheers he gives me two pills. I get the first one down with just a fleeting yet nasty taste, then I gag on the second one. The crowd cheers as I feel my stomach contract. Jed is standing right in front of me laughing, and if I do vomit I'm going to vomit all over him. He doesn't try to get out of the way. I swallow the cherry down and gag again. I pause, waiting. Jed waits too. Then he laughs and says, "No?"

I shake my head. No, not today. I move on to the hot tub, and two burley stokers lift me up and dunk me down into the lukewarm, briny, greasy water. Everything is muffled for a few seconds while my head is covered. My eyes sting, reminding me of my tear gas training.

"Clean!" the court cries out as I surface feeling about as dirty as ever. Emerging from the pool I stand around, the hot sun drying me.

There's a pause in the celebrations while all the new shellbacks are allowed to go shower. I rinse clean and follow the crowd up to the fo'c'sle in the evening for the grand entrance of Davy Jones himself. One of the combat chiefs is dressed up as Davy Jones and the xenon searchlight (we call it the Xenon Death Ray) from atop the bridge is focused on him like a stage floodlight. He gives a great speech about the lucky few who get to see this part of the world and how we all belong to one brotherhood now as shellbacks.

"Bring out the prisoners!" he bellows as the officers are paraded in front of us. They are wearing over-sized adult diapers, no pants, and baby hats. One by one King Neptune's court goes down the line and dunks containers of beans down their heads and faces or pours honey down their diapers. The baby EO, Sub-Lieutenant Finley, who is considered by many to be quite attractive, gets an entire pot of honey poured down her legs. Beyond cheering, I watch people stare and almost drool as the honey runs slowly downward.

Once the officers have all been thoroughly hazed, the ritual is called to a close and everyone breaks up to grab beers and socialize. I'm suddenly tired so I go to my rack.

SUPER-ALL-NIGHTERS

The Canadian Navy is one of the last wet navies in the world, meaning that they still allow alcohol consumption on-board. The Americans, who run a dry Navy, love our boats.

Thanks to Super-All-Nighters, two out of four nights I can get some deep sleep. I skip supper so my stomach is empty and go to the Cave when the bar opens and the beer machine gets unlocked. The beer machine is probably the most preciously guarded piece of equipment on-board. It's basically a pop machine that's been filled with cans of beer. On the older two-eighty class of ships (destroyers), the beer machine is hooked up to emergency power so in the event of a blackout the beer stays cold.

The Cave is crowded with all the ship's company who aren't working or sleeping. Everyone's socializing among themselves. No one talks to me as I feed my change into the beer machine and select Kokanee. Where else can you buy a can of beer for $1.50? I take my two beers to a crowded table and sit on the edge of the bench, drinking them as quickly as possible. The crushing anonymous crowd makes me nervous. There are so many people on-board I don't know. The longer I stay in the Cave when it's crowded the lonelier I feel because no one seems to notice that I'm there. It reminds me that people have already picked their friends, and no one seems to have picked me.

As soon as I've drunk my two beers, I put the cans in the recycling and go to my Mess. I change into my pajamas and crawl into my rack. The two beers on an empty stomach do their job quickly. I relax and my body feels heavy. Tight muscles loosen up. This is the only time I can seem to relax. I get drowsy and I have no trouble falling asleep. I sleep for up to four hours at a time which is a huge accomplishment for me while on ship. The Mess door opening and closing constantly still wakes me up, and the constant fatigue never quite goes away, but come morning I feel slightly more rested.

WINNIPEG PREPARES TO FIGHT

By now the rumours are true. We are headed to the coast of Somalia to join SNMG1, or Standing NATO Maritime Group One. We've been assigned our Box in the Gulf of Aden. Sporting our new LRAD out of Singapore, the ship goes through combat drills to make sure all our fighting might is ready. These are on top of the randomly occurring bong-bongs and daily engineering drills.

We have some new faces on-board since Singapore. One of them is WO Genette, a military photographer who gets referred to in the slang as a combat camera. She takes the last free female rack on-board, which is just below Chelsea's, which is just below mine in one Mess. We have some civvies on-board too. A handful of embedded journalists have joined the crew. I don't know where they're sleeping.

One day I'm off watch and sleeping in my rack when I'm jolted awake by a series of loud pounding noises. It sounds like someone is hitting the deckhead by my rack with a sledgehammer. I get a sudden burst of adrenaline from the surprise. I realize that the ship is firing its main gun, doing some target practice. The main gun continues to fire at random intervals and I groan, unable to get back to sleep.

I continue with my gruelling work schedule. The machinery spaces continue to terrify me when I'm down in them alone. We have a few more RASs, and now I'm qualified to stand them alone as the RAS ET. They always seem to be scheduled for times when I am supposed to be getting what little sleep I can.

During my first RAS as RAS ET alone, the RAS buffer maintains almost constant eye contact with me. He's nervous about me being able to do my job. I follow all of his commands quickly and correctly though. Just after the hose is seated in the bell and I can relax somewhat, I see dolphins jumping across the bow of the fuelling ship. This is my first time seeing dolphins in the wild, and suddenly I'm pointing and saying, "Oh look, dolphins!"

"OS Peffers, stay focused on the job at hand!" warns the RAS buffer.

I'm up on the port missile deck one afternoon in a rare break moment, trying to relax to the sound of my music. Now I find I just get tired when I relax and then I just want to go to my rack. My eyes are heavy as I sit in the equatorial sun feeling the soothing rhythm of *Winnipeg* moving through the ocean. I lose track of time and almost fall asleep. I decide to head in then and get another cup of coffee because I still have a lot of work to get done today.

I've just stepped back inside the bridge from the port bridge wing when the officer of the watch sees me. His jaw drops open, and he asks me where I was. I say I was on the port missile deck, suddenly afraid that I'm in trouble for something again. He looks a bit pale as he proceeds to tell me that they are about to have a .50-calibre firing exercise, and that the missile decks would be in the line of fire. He tells me that the port lookout had told him no one was up there. I guess the port lookout didn't look properly. Well, I think to myself, that was a close one.

I continue to work out every few days and now I'm remembering to bring my uniform with me. Robertson is nowhere to be seen for these moments.

One day I'm horsing around in the Cave with OS Ryan, and I go to grab his knife from his hip scabbard. His right hand flies to his knife but not fast enough. I've already got a grip on the handle and I'm pulling it out. As I'm pulling the blade out his hand clamps down on it and I end up slitting open the palm of his hand with his knife. He stands there for a second, staring at his palm while an angry red gash starts to bleed.

I grab a wad of napkins from the nearest table and clamp down on his hand. Then I pull him by that hand out of the Cave and up the ladder to sick bay. He still looks confused. I'm muttering an apology while I steer him down the flats to sick bay's open door. The doc sees the hand with blood already soaking into the napkins and thanks me for bringing him in. OS Ryan shrugs and laughs, saying it was an accident when the doc asks what happened.

I'm down in the forward AMR doing rounds with Holloway. There's a gushing cascade of water falling down one bulkhead quickly filling up the bilge. We head back to the MCR to report the flood, and some hull techs are dispatched. Apparently someone left a fire main open; that was the water we were seeing.

The ETs make preparations for entering our Box. Deceptive lighting is rigged so that our mast, bow, and stern appear smaller at night. The idea is to look like a small innocent fishing vessel and lure the pirates to us, so that then we can attack.

I'm on the list for a rifle shoot one afternoon on the flight deck. I stand in a line with some other junior ranks, and we pick up our rifles. We face outward and the supervising PO tells us to fire on our own time.

I cock my rifle, slam the forward assist, thumb the safety, and come up on aim. There are no targets out here. I empty my magazine into a passing wave. The PO comes up to me and warns me that I was getting too close to shooting the guardrail. I want to disagree since I always aim every shot I make, and all I could see through my scope was water. Instead I reply with a "Sorry, PO."

On watch I'm left alone now. I sit and work on my packages or do lamp-ups. The ETOW goes off and does maintenance alone. I'm in the MCR practicing flipping through the various electrical screens as quickly as possible when Donalds turns around, "OS Peffers," he says.

I stand up to get a better look at him. It's getting hard to hear orders now because of a large droning air conditioning unit sitting in the corner by my console. It's on all the time now. He motions me to come around to his console. I do that, and he hands me his empty coffee mug.

"Fill'er up with cream and sugar from the Cave." I turn to leave the MCR to go do his bidding, and I hear him say, "Thanks, doll."

I come back to the MCR with Donalds's coffee in hand and find him in mid-sentence talking to a few other PO 2 stokers who have accumulated.

"You do realize that that's piss, right? You're getting a face full of piss. I won't do it. Once was enough. And I mean my wife stinks like fish, and so when she farts her farts smell like fish…"

I close my eyes and shake my head and become very absorbed with my console. Another alarm comes in for DG2 stage one enclosure leak.

I'm heading forward on two deck one day, and I start to head down one of the steeper ladders on ship leading to three deck. Suddenly in midstride the ship lurches violently and I'm catapulted off the ladder. I'm in free fall, and I reach up with my hands scrabbling at the deckhead for any kind of purchase. I grab onto a pipe, and I hang there for a few seconds, grateful for my upper body strength. The ship smooths out again, and I drop down onto three deck. I look around and see no one. No one saw me almost wipe out. I continue walking, and *Winnipeg* continues her rhythmic bucking.

I'm in the Cave by myself at one of the tables, working on one of my electrical drawings when I hear our usual engine drone suddenly cut out. I hear the pipe for the MCR response team, and the engineering officer of the watch's voice sounds slightly panicked. Something big has just broken, I think. I head to the MCR to check it out. A small party of grim-faced stokers are making their way down into the AER as I'm making my way aft on three deck. I discover that a cylinder temperature in the PDE has gone through the roof. It's not long before the damage report comes in. Multiple cylinders are found to be defective. The on- watch stoker explains to me that we can no longer use our PDE. It's just the two GTs that have the job of propelling us through the rest of our deployment.

ACTION

I'm peddling a stationary bike at 0800 in the CO's flats, getting in a quick morning workout before my watch starts. I'm peddling and smiling to myself as the morning wakey-wakey song plays throughout the ship: Toto's "Africa."

The XO comes on the shincom then, "Good morning, *Winnipeg*, and welcome to our first day in SNMG1, or Standing NATO Maritime Group One, and the Horn of Africa in the Arabian Sea."

His tone of voice is light and hopeful. There's an energy going around the crew, I can feel it. We're finally doing what we've been waiting for through three months of routine manoeuvres, diplomatic missions, and training scenarios. This is it, this is what we spend our whole careers training for: Operational Deployment.

I remember that excitement, feeling hope for my future. I'm lucky to be here. This will make my young career look good. I'm up and coming. I'm going somewhere. We're all so important; you can tell by the embedded journalists and the camera crew, by our fully loaded guns and the coffin cargo strapped to the bulkhead in the hangar. We are a force to be reckoned with, and we want a piece of the action. We are a hungry shark prowling our hunting grounds.

I'm standing on the bridge by the bosunmate's desk. I'm excited when I hear a distress call come in over the radio. I'm about to start to make my way to my section base in anticipation of the action stations the captain is about to order. I pause, then I'm confused. Things aren't happening the way they're supposed to.

No one is moving fast enough. The nav comm has his head in his hands. The bosunmate's hands, which should be pressing buttons on the shincom and holding the pipe that lies discarded on the desk, are drumming restlessly on the desk's Plexiglas surface. The CO and the XO are talking in hushed tones between themselves in their chairs.

There's a horrible voice on the radio that I will never forget.

"NATO 338, NATO 338…please respond NATO 338…"

The voice is begging over and over for us to respond. There's a tight constricted desperation in the voice that I've never heard before and I haven't heard since. This voice is afraid for its life, and you can hear the fear.

The captain continues his dialogue and reaches up to his radio at the deckhead above his chair and turns down the volume of that voice.

"What the hell is going on? Why aren't we responding?" I'm asking these questions to the tired-looking bosunmate. He simply tells me, "We're too far away." He goes on, "In order to maintain our fuel supply, we are only responding to distress calls that occur very close to us."

Somebody neglected to factor in the extra fuel needed to speed through the hundreds of kilometres of water we are supposed to be protecting. Somebody decided that it's more important to have fuel than to speed to the rescue.

"We would arrive minutes or hours later," the bosunmate continues, "and the pirate's hijacking would be completed and the captured vessel moved to a new location, and our fuel tanks would be empty. If we were to follow NATO's rules of engagement and respond, we would end up dead in the water, waiting on refuelling…"

Refuelling is strictly scheduled around the task group.

"In the middle of an empty part of the ocean, of no use to anyone," the bosunmate explains this to me while the voice begs in the background. We are not a shark, and we don't go hunting. Instead we are a spider stuck in its web, cursed with waiting.

We can't even acknowledge their distress call because maritime law says that if you acknowledge a distress call you are bound to respond to that distress call. So we can't even tell them we've heard them.

"How many?" I ask. "How many distress calls are we getting? How often does this happen?" I only visit the bridge for a few minutes every other day.

"Half a dozen to a dozen a day," he tells me wearily.

He's stuck at his post, they all are. And they can't shut the radio off. They're forced to listen. A terrible thick silence fills the bridge while everyone listens to the poor voice pleading for help. I'm just standing. Time seems to stop. The beauty of the endless sun and sparkling blue ocean makes no sense here. My gaze lowers until I'm staring at the deck. First I feel disbelief, then shock, then a spreading numbness. Something inside me is curling up, shutting down, turning away.

"We've been boarded!" The voice goes up half an octave in desperation, "Oh my God, they're right on top of us!"

Soon it'll be over. I now feel nothing, and I don't want to hear anymore. My legs move mechanically as I walk toward the door. The bridge isn't my post; I can leave whenever I want. I want to go deep down inside *Winnipeg* now. I don't remember leaving the bridge, but I must have since now I'm standing in the Cave pouring myself a cup of coffee.

ET PHONE HOME

I put off what I want to do most. I have some free time, and I go up to the bridge flats just aft of the chart room. There are four satellite phones rigged up here, two in the flats and two in adjacent compartments. It's normal to see people sitting in the flats cradling a phone to their shoulder. It's a sad sight to see people missing the ones they love. Some people just sit in silence, listening. Some people cry. Some people try to talk. There isn't much to say though when every day is the same. I'm used to carefully stepping over people while they are half a world away on my way to the chart room or bridge.

I don't call home very often. It's a painful experience since I've been gone for almost two years now. I go through my days tired and busy but relieved because I don't often think about home now. I do a mental calculation and adjust for time zones and decide now is better than never. I take my turn sitting in the flats looking depressed. I pick up the receiver and dial the familiar number and suddenly I'm hearing a loved familiar voice again.

"Hello," Roy says.

"Hi, it's me."

"Hello, how's it going?"

"Good I suppose…"

"I'd ask you where you are, but I know you can't tell me…"

"Yeah, it's a secret."

"So…how's the weather?" Roy asks after a long pause.

"Hot…it's nice," I pause before continuing, "how's the weather in Edmonton?"

"Hot also, dry, not much rain."

There's a long pause where I don't know what else to say, and I wait for Roy to say something. Finally he asks, "So, how is your training going?"

"Good, I guess." I think back to all the reprimands I've received and decide it's too complicated and depressing to tell Roy about it right now.

"How do you like all the foreign ports?"

"They're interesting… I like exploring all the sights."

There's another long pause as I sit cradling the receiver to my head. The silence gets awkward. I don't know what else to say.

"I miss you," Roy's voice sounds small.

I sit with my back to the bulkhead, cradling the phone to my shoulder, feeling awful. Someone carefully steps over me on their way to the bridge. I get the words out: "I miss you too…I love you." A painful lump fills my throat, and I try to swallow it away.

There's another long pause, then Roy continues, "I have to push back the date for when I move out to the Island again."

"Oh." My voice sounds small too.

"There's a new deadline at work, the project is getting extended."

"I see." My heart aches then as I sit on the deck feeling miserable.

"Now it looks like I can move in December." Before it was September, and before that it was spring, just before I started the deployment.

I don't know what to say while I absorb this latest bit of news. I miss him so much then that my knees start to tremble. Thankfully I'm already sitting on the deck. I hug myself protectively and swallow again and again while the lump in my throat makes me speechless. After a while Roy speaks, "Are you still there?"

"Yes." My voice sounds tight as I speak through the painful lump in my throat.

Roy seems to be weathering our separation better than me. The soul-crushing loneliness that I try my best to ignore doesn't seem to be as big an issue for him.

Silence stretches out. We've run out of things to say to each other, and now I'm just dreading the part where I know I'll have to hang up.

"I love you and miss you," Roy tells me. I can hear the emotion in his voice.

Tears start running down my face and I wipe them away with my uniform jacket sleeve. There's a deep pain in the centre of my chest.

"I love you and miss you too." My voice shakes.

There is another long pause where we are both silent.

Then I say, "Well, I guess this is goodbye again for a while."

"Okay…goodbye," Roy says gently.

"Goodbye." I am frozen holding the receiver to my ear, unable to hang up. We say goodbye to each other again and again, and I almost have to get angry in order to push myself to put the receiver back in its cradle. The phone call is over, and I'm left curled up on the deck hugging the satellite phone.

I sit there feeling completely drained. With this new timeline we will have been exactly two years apart. I can't do this much longer. Everyone has their limits. I sit and feel the rhythmic motion of the deck, and it soothes me. I take some deep breaths and start to plan what I'll work on next in my training package. Slowly I return to *Winnipeg*. There's work to be done, things to learn, a PO 1 to please, machinery to be terrified of, and a ship that seems to be slowly breaking. I get to my feet, leaning heavily against the bulkhead. I wipe my nose on my sleeve. My uniform seems to absorb all kinds of things. Sweat, blood, tears, snot. And it never seems to leave a mark.

TENSION ON THE LINE

Now that our PDE is out of service we're using our GTs all the time now. We run just one at low speed for cruising, and when we have to go full speed we start the other one and run them both all out. This means we're using more fuel so we start RASing more frequently. Each time I spend hours standing with the winch controller in my hand.

One RAS, we're fuelling at night with a Central American tanker. Red lighting and glow sticks are all the light we can use. It starts to go badly. The spanwire is connected, and the heavy bundle of hoses starts to get hauled over under the power of our winch and by extension my fingers pressing the buttons on the winch controller. A large amount of tension develops on the rope, and I quickly notice that the line is all tangled up in the hoses. I follow the commands from the RAS buffer, and he orders me to heave in slowly this time. More and more tension develops on the line until it's pulled taut around the drum of the winch and a stretching noise starts to come from the rope.

We continue to heave in, and the stretching noise turns to a popping noise. The rope is so tight now it looks thinner. I feel like that rope, tight with tension. The bosuns start to back away from the popping, tight line, and then I know it's not safe. I can't move though; I'm tethered to the winch by the controller in my hands. I start to feel very exposed and uncomfortable. My eyes are glued to the RAS buffer, and he's dividing his attention between the line and me.

Back before my first RAS, when I was gathering the RAS supplies from the shop, MS Hampton told me the story of a RAS ET who died back in the nineties when a welded eyelet on the deck gave out because of a bad weld. The block and tackle exploded outward from the sudden release of tension and hit the RAS ET square in the face, killing him instantly.

I glance wide-eyed now at that eyelet as the rope feeding through it gets tighter and tighter. The tension mounts even further, and everyone is backing away. I'm now the closest person to the line. My heart is pounding. My thumb starts to ride the stop button, pressing it in to where I can feel the contactor in the controls. The RAS buffer barks a stop command, and I have the line stopped so fast he's still barking the command while it stops. He yells his next command to me to heave in slowly again, and I cringe inwardly as I press the controls. The hose only has a few more feet to travel. It's almost there, but the line is fit to break soon. More popping noises come from an even thinner line now.

Over the next few minutes I'm ordered to start and stop again over and over while the hose inches slowly closer. The tension fills my entire body, which I don't see as mine anymore. The hands and fingers belong to the buffer. The legs and torso are only there to support the hands and fingers. I'm just another expendable deck fitting. Just an extension of the winch controller. If the line breaks, I just hope it's over quickly.

Time seems to stop or drag out to infinity. The line pops menacingly, and I stare helplessly at the RAS buffer. My fingers have never moved so fast as I carry out his commands. The tension is screaming inside me, and then finally he barks a stop command. With just another foot to go for the bell, the RAS buffer decides it's too dangerous to continue. He orders me to check away slowly, and bit by bit the line relaxes and swells to its normal size again. The horrible popping noises stop, and the rest of the RAS party resumes their places around me.

The lines are sent back. We manoeuvre ourselves to the other side of the tanker, and we use the starboard RAS equipment instead. This time the line they send over isn't tangled. It's not long before the hose is seated in the bell and we're taking on fuel as normal. This RAS takes twice as long as a normal RAS, and most of the people working it have been swapped out with fresh bodies from their departments. No one comes to relieve me, though.

When the RAS is finished and we're breaking away, I gather up the winch controller and its cord, wrap it in a coil, and sling it over my shoulder. I'm stepping over the dump, and I pass the RAS buffer. It's MS Monro, who seems to be the best RAS buffer. He pauses from giving orders to get my attention. "OS Peffers, you did really well today," he tells me.

"Thank you, Master Seaman," I say, feeling a bit of pride again. If only someone could tell that to my department.

Most of the RASs are carried out with no incident, but one day as we're just releasing the spanwire and the heavy weight of hoses is being dragged backward across the deck and then down into the choppy waters between us and the tanker, the bosun who released the spanwire suddenly realizes he's caught on the line. He has mere seconds to react before he's swept overboard and hauled through the water. He works frantically to free himself, and the RAS buffer pulls a six-inch hunting knife from his belt, ready to cut the line. He gets free of the line, and then it's gone over the side. He sighs with relief, and the buffer puts his knife away.

WARNING SHOTS

Now that we're in our Box, every morning once the wakey-wakey song has been played and Jed is finished with his weather report and joke, the XO comes on the shincom and updates us about the pirates. "Good morning, *Winnipeg*, here's the update on the piracy situation. As of last night there have been three new attacks…"

Hijackings, kidnappings, ransoms. There's a growing sense of frustration building in me as I listen. All we do is circle our Box while the distress calls pour in. I start to long for some action.

We've been in our Box for days now. We're sucked into a black hole of disorienting timelessness so I don't know how many days it's been. Finally we get a distress call we can respond to. The helo is launched to intercept, and I hear the hydraulic start pack spool up to start the other GT. A low rumbling thunder permeates the ship, and the bulkheads start to vibrate as we come up on full speed. We're in hot pursuit for hours. I'm in my rack trying to get some sleep when the XO comes on the pipe: "Good evening. We're pursuing the pirates, and currently warning shots from the helo have failed. We're going to intercept them. This is a ten-minute warning. We will go to action stations in ten minutes. That is all."

Everyone on-board is suddenly jacked up on adrenaline. I go to the Heads and brush my teeth and slip a few DVDs into the forward section base. All around me are war whoops, and people quoting action movies with lines like: "Get some!" and "Shit just got real!"

I join the steady stream of traffic moving through the flats as the entire ship wakes up and prepares for a fight.

I'm in the forward section base stepping into my too-big bunker gear along with the rest of the attack team as I hear the motor for the main gun whine to life directly above us. As planned, bong-bongs sound throughout the ship. It's a flurry of activity—and then we're all sitting in the weapons tech shop waiting. The bunker gear is hot, and water bottles are passed around.

I can't stand to just sit and do nothing. There's a powerful restlessness seizing me. I pick a DVD from my case and stick it in the DVD player. *The Mummy*, starring Brendan Fraser, begins to play. The section base buffer doesn't mind so long as we keep the volume down so we can hear the XO's updates. The movie starts to play, and all our adrenaline-infused attention focuses on the screen.

MS Earle is sitting right next to me on comms with the weapons tech on the bridge. He's leaning into me, his shoulder applying gentle pressure to mine. I find myself looking around, checking eyes. Everyone is rapt, wide-eyed and waiting.

The minutes stretch on and finally the XO tells us, "We're approaching the pirate vessel." His tone of voice is almost bored, he sounds that calm. "We are giving warning shots now."

I hear the .50-calibre gun firing, and someone calls down about the movie from the couch "Turn it up!" Everyone laughs a little too loudly.

"This is it people!" the section base buffer calls out from his station in the adjacent compartment. Warning shots have failed. The rules of engagement tell us we can now shoot to kill except when the enemy is running away. I have a singular moment of awareness as we come to the very brink.

The XO tells us, "We are engaging the LRAD now," and I hear a whistle that sounds much like a car alarm.

A few seconds later the XO is on the pipe again. "The pirates have lost control of their vessel; we are closing to intercept." The drone from the engines dies down as *Winnipeg* slows quickly.

"We have the pirates in custody now," the XO tells us, a slight urgency creeping into his otherwise calm voice.

Over the next few hours *Winnipeg* is gradually stood down from action stations while the CO argues with bureaucrats in Ottawa. I'm allowed to take off my sweaty bunker gear, and the section base drains of people. JD comes to find me.

"Hey, Peff, come help troubleshoot UPS #7 with me," he says.

UPS #7 just happens to be on the bridge. We climb up onto a crowded dark bridge, and I come to a standstill with my mouth hanging open at the scene in front of me.

Just off our port bow is a small boat with three people in it. They're all standing with their arms held high over their heads. They aren't holding their arms up like you see in the movies, but rather they appear to be reaching upward as high as possible, as if they couldn't raise their arms high enough. They are staring up at us, or rather they would be staring if they could see. Our Xenon Death Ray is aimed right at them, and all its millions of candelas have them bathed in the brightest white light I've ever seen. All colour is drained in this intense beam. The water and sky are pitch black, and the people standing before us are a brilliant white. Their black skin is white. Their thin frames are white. Their ragged clothing is white. I watch their eyes as they continue to dart about nervously.

The xenon search light on top of the bridge is classified as a weapon. It's very useful for blinding people. It requires so much power that it's the only light I've ever seen that's hooked up to 440V power. The three people before us are completely and utterly at our mercy. I continue to stare. They have nothing with them. They dumped their weapons overboard long ago. They are no longer pirates. I see three desperately poor people desperate to remain alive and at this moment wondering if they are about to be killed. Our main gun is still trained on them. Our .50-calibre guns are still trained on them. We tower before them with our god-like power. Three-quarter-inch steel in all its glory.

I look again at their boat. They have nothing. Absolutely nothing. We must appear like kings in front of them with our cushy seats and racks, our hot water and our hot meals. Our lives waiting for us back home with our houses and cars and bank cards. Our fancy weapon that uses sound waves. They're lucky the Canadians caught them. If the Americans (who are operating outside of NATO) had caught them, they would most likely have been shot.

"Hey, Peff," JD whispers to me and the spell is broken. I turn to see JD standing next to me, ushering me over to the starboard side of the bridge, over to UPS #7. We make a show of pressing a few buttons on the device, checking it in various places for excessive heat, and then finally we have no further reason to be on the bridge.

Dazed and blinking afterimages from my eyes in the darkness, I follow him back below decks. Is this really happening? I'm suddenly seized by a strong sugar craving bordering on nausea. I go to the Cave, feeling very strange. I take out a mug and mix myself some hot chocolate. I sit at a table sipping the hot, sweet liquid. The sugar hits my stomach, and I start feeling better. I look around and see LS Lonsdale hunched over the counter with a beer in his hand. He's shaking as he lifts the can to drink. He's talking to his buddies and telling them about how it was him doing the warning shots.

The combat camera and journalists go to work now as the XO gives another pipe.

"Good evening, *Winnipeg*. We've been ordered to release the pirates, so that is exactly what we're going to do. Good work everyone on the capture; you've made your country proud tonight."

Laptops are connected to satellite feeds, and the whole story hits the press in a matter of hours. We'll make the morning news back in Canada.

FIGURING IT OUT

It's the Mids watch, and cleaning stations are under way. All the cleaning in the MCR happens during the Mids and Morning watches and is carried out by the stoker and ET watchkeepers and roundsmen. I carry a bucket with warm soapy water and a sponge from the cleaning gear locker up forward through the dark-red flats aft to the MCR. When I get back in the MCR, Donalds talks to the stoker roundsmen: "Go take a break in the Cave."

Donalds looks at me next. "OS Peffers, start scrubbing the deck."

I go to work washing the deck. With everyone gone from the MCR except for Donalds, the DC watchkeeper, and the one on-watch stoker, there aren't people standing or sitting around getting in my way. I start in the corner of the compartment and work backward on my knees until the entire deck has been cleaned. The usual soundtrack plays in the background. Alarms sound. The air conditioner drones in the corner. The DC watchkeeper turns the page in a magazine.

Once the deck is done, Donalds glances over to me and speaks again: "OS Peffers, wash down the consoles now."

I grab the spray bottle and the paper towel from the sink in the corner and go about wiping down the console screens and keyboards. The watchkeepers get up and move politely out of my way while I work.

I find Donalds watching me while I finish off the last console. He says, "Have you figured it out yet?"

"Figured out what yet?" I reply. I'm confused and anxious again.

"You're being punished," he tells me, "you're doing all the cleaning stations by yourself tonight."

Guilt weighs heavily on me again on top of the confusion. I can't seem to avoid getting in trouble no matter how hard I try. I stand there for a while, trying to phrase my next words.

"What have I done?" I ask carefully.

"It's your attitude that needs improving," Donalds tells me sternly.

I feel irritation. "What about my attitude needs improvement?" I know it sounds like a challenge.

"Stop talking back and questioning me and go take out the gash!" he tells me angrily.

I stand there still. Words fill my mouth. Finally I say, "If you intend to punish me in the future, please tell me in advance what I'm being punished for so that I know what to change in the future." I turn my back, walk over to the gash in the corner, and start to gather it up. I'm hauling the bag out the door when I hear Donalds say, offhandedly, "I'll do that."

I close the inside door in the CO's airlock and open the outer door. Warm humid night air greets me as I haul the gash aft to the dry gash compartment. There's a quicker way to get there from inside *Winnipeg* but I want some air so I go the long way through the upper decks. Light discipline is strongly enforced, and I don't have a red light flashlight. I notice it's pitch-black out here since there's no moon tonight. I keep one hand trailing along the hull as I walk carefully.

Suddenly I collide with something solid and stumble backward.

"Sorry," I hear someone say close by, and I realize I've run into another person. I feel a light touch on my shoulder as they pass by me in the darkness. I have no idea who it was.

I spend the rest of the watch doing the lamp-ups that no one else wants to do, the ones with the ballasts. I thought maybe tonight I would like to pound and shove bits of metal, but I just find myself getting even more frustrated.

Finally I'm done, and I meet a tired-looking Pellier in the MCR for the changeover. I've learned the code the ETOWs have been using to communicate the state of the ship. I tell him, "Two and three, one, two, starboard, starboard, number two." The first two numbers are which generators are running. The next one is which fire pump is running. Next is the HP air compressor, the two lube oil pumps that are on, and which steering pump is being used. He nods groggily to me and sits down at the console, automatically flipping through the screens the way we've all been shown.

On my way to my Mess up forward, I pass by the galley and it smells like baking sugar. I stick my head in the doorway and see one of the cooks is baking cupcakes to some softly playing rock music. He's just adding the icing now. He sees me and offers me one. I've been getting more sugar cravings lately, and my mouth waters at the thought of eating a fresh cupcake. I pick one from the tray and thank him. I walk on and notice the decoration on the cupcake. It's a chocolate cupcake with white icing covering it, then traced over the white is a thin ribbon of red icing in the shape of a cartoon penis and balls. I laugh to myself as I take a sugar-filled bite.

By the time I get up the next day rumours have spread throughout the ship that there are genital cupcakes in the duff tray. Duff is Navy slang for baked goods. Rumours spread quickly that some officers found out and disapproved. The cooks are ordered to remove the offending frosting. By the time I get to the galley for breakfast, all that's left are a bunch of cupcakes with scrape marks on them.

I hear *Winnipeg* speed up again as I sit by myself in the Cave working on my package. We turn sharply and I quickly and coolly grab my coffee mug as it begins to slide off the table. I've lost track of how many cups I've had today. I'm starting to feel jittery and tired at the same time.

The XO comes on the pipe again: "Good afternoon, *Winnipeg*. We're in pursuit of more suspected pirates. I'll keep you updated as the situation develops. That is all."

I think back to our last successful capture sometime in the timeless past of more than a few days ago. The next day the journalists left a copy of their article in the Cave. I had read it and was appalled at the inaccuracy. There was no mention of the LRAD. Instead, *Winnipeg* had caught them with her "superior manoeuvring abilities." This is the first time in my life that I've been involved with something newsworthy before it gets to the news, and I wonder why the public can't know about the LRAD. I sit there feeling a deep sense of betrayal. I've always heard accusations that the press gets things wrong; I've just never been in a position to have such an obvious example until now.

After about half an hour of hot pursuit, we come to boarding stations. The pipe echoes throughout the ship.

I hear people milling through the flats quickly. As a member of the engineering department, I don't respond to these. The boarding party, which usually closes up on the couches in the Cave with their full swat gear, suddenly jump up and file out into the flats.

Winnipeg slows quickly again, and the XO comes on the pipe again: "Good afternoon, *Winnipeg*. We have the vessel in custody."

A few minutes later I hear the XO again, only his tone of voice is upbeat. "The vessel we've captured is full of refugees, women and children on their way to Yemen. We are dispensing food, water, and medical attention. Good work, *Winnipeg*."

Just before I go on watch, I meet Alders in the Heads. She's peeling off her ship's diver's outfit and chatting to Race Car. They were both on the boarding party. Alders had been the token female soldier handing bottles of water to the poor Africans for the combat camera. It makes the news the next day, and this time there's video footage.

That evening, during my workout, I remember thinking back to the refugees and feeling pride in our ability to help.

Time stretches on, and we fire up the GTs to chase more pirates. This time they get away. And the next. Days go by with no action. I think it stretches into weeks, but I'm not sure. I'm in the chart room with Jed. I've started bringing up cups of green tea, and now we sit sipping tea with music in the background. It's been a while since I've been to the chart room although I couldn't say exactly how long. Long enough to get an update from Jed about what's happening on ship.

"Want to know what I was doing while we captured those pirates earlier?" Jed asks, a hint of sarcasm already in his voice.

"Okay, what were you doing?" I smile.

"I was in the prestigious position of eating a muffin," he laughs.

"I was sitting in my section base watching a movie," I say in reply.

"Yup, eating a muffin, real combat that was."

"At least you weren't closed up in sweaty bunker gear."

"Eww, that stuff gets so stinky after a deployment."

There's a lull in the conversation then as we sip our teas thoughtfully.

Jed pipes up again: "The CO is getting quite frustrated with all the distress calls that we can't do anything about." I think back to the distress call that I overheard on the bridge earlier and feel for the CO.

"He had wanted to scuttle the pirate dhow that we caught earlier, but Ottawa wouldn't let him," Jed continues. "The other day when I was on the bridge, we got another distress call. The CO just got up from his chair and left the bridge."

One day a pirate's dhow is captured by the boarding party, and the small vessel has a fuel leak from its engine. The pirates have no shoes and are standing in diesel, which has burned their feet. The boarding party complains about their ruined boots.

I find myself in the chart room again with Jed. I bring more green tea.

"What was Afghanistan like?" I ask out of curiosity.

Jed snorts dismissively.

"Boredom and repetition," he tells me. "Like this. Although I did have an espresso machine in Camp Mirage."

Finally *Winnipeg* gets to do something again. I don't know how long it's been. We've been tasked to escort the World Food Programme ship along its voyage into Mogadishu, Somalia. Down in the MCR, Donalds is waving his hand dismissively about the bucket of rust we're escorting.

"They can only do twelve knots as their best speed!" he says.

We're following faithfully behind them at twelve knots.

Escort missions are boring. We're guaranteed no action. It's just hours of sailing. I don't mind it though. I figure at least we're doing something good. It's better than just circling our Box ignoring distress calls. I go up to the bridge to get a better look. I have to spend a few minutes squinting painfully in the bright sunlight now. I've been avoiding the bridge since I overheard that distress call. I spend so much time down below now that sunlight is too bright. I hug my pole, rest my tired head against cool metal, and wait for my eyes to adjust.

The officer of the watch tells a different side of the story. "The World Food Programme picks old breaking ships because they are the cheapest, and that way they can buy more rice and ultimately feed more people."

Hearing it like that it makes logical sense. I stand up forward by the bridge windows holding the wooden railing, watching a ship on the horizon billowing black exhaust into a brilliant blue sky.

Engineering drills continue every afternoon, but for now we aren't doing bong-bongs. Since we're in the Box, any bong-bongs will signify the real thing. I respond for more steering gear breakdowns, and I'm told to move faster although if I move any faster I'll be running. You never ever run on ship, no matter the emergency. The chances of tripping and falling and breaking your face are just too great.

One day during drills I'm sitting at my console and I don't hear an order from the engineering officer of the watch. Donalds barks at me: "Wake up!"

"OS Peffers, you really need to listen up during drills," the EO tells me oh so kindly.

"The problem is the air..." I start to explain.

"OS Peffers, you don't talk back when the EO is talking to you," Donalds is quick to tell me.

The next day during drills (which aren't even when I'm on watch, but Robertson expects me to take part in them every day for practice) I feel a sudden stab of irritation for fat, sweaty Donalds, and I think I hear my name but I'm not sure over the din. I quickly reach up and switch off the air conditioner—and sure enough I'm being ordered to remotely turn on a fuel pump motor. I quickly thumb through the pages on my console and mouse over the pump, pressing the required buttons.

"The fuel pump is running!" I say over the noise in the room. Before the debrief Donalds orders me to turn the air conditioner back on.

The air conditioner wars continue between Donalds and me until finally one day during the debrief while the EO is giving me feedback, I blurt out: "I can't hear a damn thing with the AC on!"

His handsome face looks surprised, and he says "Oh," as if he finally gets something.

He turns to Donalds then and tells him, "During drills we will have the air conditioner turned off."

Donalds replies the only way he can, which is to say, "Yes, sir."

I have a small private victory moment while the EO sides with me.

It's the Afternoon watch, and I'm on with Stafford. The lamp-ups are done so I'm in my corner of the MCR with my training package while Stafford does a Sudoku puzzle. I steal a jealous glance around the MCR. Two stoker roundsmen are sitting on the deck chatting. The DC watchkeeper is reading a magazine. Donalds has his laptop out resting on top of his console, and he's watching a TV show with very low volume. No one else is working. I long to have someone talk to me. I'm basically ignored by everyone except Jed. The luxury of reading a magazine or just sitting and chatting seems so comforting. I'm making good progress on my package though. In about a month I will have completed everything I can do while the ship is sailing. I'm starting to hate the work though, because it's all I'm ever allowed to do.

A high-pitched alarm comes in, and the on-watch stoker yells, "Flame sensor on DG2!"

I turn in my chair and watch as Donalds is adjusting the CCTV footage to show the forward AMR.

"ET, send a start to number one!" Donalds calls out, and Stafford is already pressing buttons. The CCTV footage shows wisps of smoke rising from the generator. "Put number one on load and emergency stop number two!" Donalds yells. Then he's gone from the MCR faster than I thought possible for him to move.

Stafford puts the standby generator on load and shuts down DG2. I see Donalds through the camera down in the forward AMR with a few stokers throwing off the enclosure doors. More smoke billows out, Donalds is spraying a CO_2 fire extinguisher at the machinery. Within seconds the fire seems to be out, and DG2 sits silently.

We just had a fire. The DC watchkeeper is watching from her chair, but no one has raised the alarm. No one besides the stokers and ETs find out about the fire.

After the investigation it turns out there was a fuel leak on DG2, and the leaking fuel is what was burning. The generator is put back on load but continues to have flame-like symptoms so finally it's locked out. We're down another generator. Now *Winnipeg* is running on DG1 and DG3, our two remaining generators.

One day I'm called into the shop by Robertson while I'm on watch, and I see Alders standing there waiting for me as well. I want to disappear as the door is closed, and I'm trapped again in the tiny space with two people I can't seem to ever please.

"I'm disappointed, OS Peffers, with your recent emails I've been monitoring," Robertson tells me with his arms across his chest, his voice dripping with disapproval. "It's going on your div notes that you're not addressing people appropriately in those emails," he continues.

"If the person is of a higher rank than you, you must from now on address them with 'Hello, sir' or 'Hello' followed by the appropriate rank," he explains. "A simple 'Hi' is not good enough. Secondly, you need to stop referring to Master Seaman Alders as Beth [her first name] while we are in chain-of-command scenarios, and Alders wishes you to call her Beth when outside of chain-of-command scenarios." Robertson goes on, "Basic Training is over, and people do not like being referred to simply by their last names."

Alders stands leaning against the counter, her eyes bore icily into mine. I swallow my sudden burst of anger and feel my face flush with heat. All I can do is say, "Yes, PO."

NATURAL BEAUTY

Alders stands in front of her mirror, again wearing just a sports bra and combat pants. She's examining her mascara wand. Her body is as stunning as usual, but her face looks gaunt and there are dark circles under her eyes.

"It took sixteen hours to troubleshoot and fix the dryer for #2 HP air compressor," she tells me tiredly.

I lather my shampoo with my hands, working it through my hair. I feel nothing for her except a nasty sense of pleasure at seeing her suffer. "That's tough," I manage to sound sincere, and my eyebrows knit together to form a sorry facial expression. I glimpse this mask briefly in my mirror before I dunk my head under the tap again.

I feel selfish, exhausted, and dirty as I towel dry my hair and comb it, like a robot, into the same style as usual. I've lost track of all the little talks we've had over my perceived behaviour problems. I know she's just following orders by doing them, that it's coming from Robertson, but it's her face I have to look at during the talks, and so it's her that I start to feel resentment toward.

Another time, it's crowded in the Heads. I'm unlucky, catching the day workers during a shift change. All around me, jostling for a corner of mirror to see themselves in, are a bunch of irritable, tired women all trying to look pretty. They dab makeup over their sunken eyes and style their bed-head hair and look even more irritated when it goes back to being lopsided again. I feel their eyes upon me as I take up a coveted space in front of a mirror. I see the scorn from eyes quickly cast away, but slow enough for me to notice. They look at me with contempt.

I had told myself I was imagining things. That my fatigue was creating paranoia. But then months after the deployment was over and we were back home again and people could get all their personal needs met like sleep and privacy, Chelsea told me the reason why everyone hated me on the deployment.

"It's your youth and natural beauty," she had said. I had given her an incredulous look. She went on, "You didn't have to try to look good. You can just roll out of your rack and give yourself a quick bird bath in the sink and look beautiful while everyone else has to spend precious minutes putting on makeup when they could have been sleeping."

My hunch that the other women on-board did not like me had been correct, but I never would have guessed the reason.

COLD SHOWERS

In an attempt to avoid the crowds, I am doing as many of my workouts as possible at night now. I just got off the Mids watch, and now I'm jogging on a treadmill on two deck outside the engineering office. My world is bathed in dark-red light, and I slip into a disorienting feeling while I run on the same treadmill to the same music over and over again. I've lost track of how many times I've done this. I don't know how long we've been at sea for now, but it seems like I've already lived a lifetime here.

A few people pass me while doing rounds, a metal triangle dangling from each of their belts. I run and feel tired. I try to not watch the digital clock on the treadmill countdown how much longer I have. I run, and Donalds is walking past me heading aft. He glances over at me, and his gait falters. He slows his walk right down and stares straight at me while he passes by as slowly as possible. I'm suddenly aware of the sweat running down my body in the equatorial heat as well as my choice of clothing—which is a tank top and shorts. I glare angrily in the low light while I run and try to ignore his eyes.

My workout is finally done, and I'm wiping down the machine with a cloth. Suddenly Donalds appears as I'm about to head forward to the showers. He blocks my path and starts to talk.

"Your training progress…it's progressing…" he mumbles. All the while his eyes stare unabashedly at my breasts. I stare back at him incredulously. He isn't even trying to hide his prying gaze. My arm shoots out and I reach for a cold metal pipe and hold on to *Winnipeg*. She moves gently beneath me. I feel trapped. I don't want to be here anymore. The sexual tension has been on the rise, and I've been trying to ignore the way people stare when they think I don't notice. I am exposed, skewered.

Finally he clears his throat, and I don't know how much time has passed while I cling to the *Winnipeg* while he gets his fill of me. But now he's moving on, and I'm left alone in the dark-red flats. This is the last day I wear a tank top on-board ship. From now on its baggy t-shirts.

I strip naked in the Heads which are empty now because it's the middle of the night between watches, and I quickly slip into the shower. I want to be washed clean but instead the water is cold. We're supposed to only have "Navy showers" while sailing. But right now, with no one watching me, I indulge in the luxury of letting the water run. It runs and runs and at best becomes lukewarm. I swear and shiver while I wash as quickly as possible.

The next day when I show up for work at 0800, the forward hot water heater has been added to the ET's list of broken equipment.

"OS Holloway and OS JD, take a look at the forward hot water heater. Basic troubleshooting, you know the drill," MS Hampton tells them. He turns to me then. "OS Peffers, clean the shop."

Holloway, JD, and I all have the same level of training, but I'm told to clean instead of help troubleshoot. I stubbornly continue to try to learn though, and once the shop is clean I head down to the forward AMR to see how the repairs are progressing. There's a partial ground on the element, and we need to order a replacement. Until then the female Heads get cold showers. I think if there's any justice on this boat it should be the male Heads aft that should be getting the cold showers.

As our time in the Box stretches on, *Winnipeg* herself seems to complain. Her bilge slowly accumulates a myriad of daily drippings from all her machinery. Leaking coolant, sea water, and diesel form the base of this soup as it slowly fills up toward the catwalks. One of the grey water tanks rusts through one day, and the hull techs have to dump its contents into the bilge. Now on top of the diesel and the warm metallic tang of rust, there's a sickly rotten egg smell coming from the bilge water.

BAD NEWS ICE CREAM

I'm about to go on watch for the Last Dogs, and I notice the cooks and mollies bringing large vats of ice cream up from the fridge flats.

The XO makes a pipe then: "Good evening. We've been at sea now for thirty days straight. It's time to have a bit of a reward. It's time for you all to enjoy some well-deserved ice cream."

I feel relief because this means we will be making port soon. Thirty days in the Box, that was the deal. A line begins to form down the flats, and I join it. People are shaking their heads and looking irritable or disappointed.

I overhear a conversation in front of me: "There's bad news coming now."

"Yeah, the ice cream only comes out right before bad news."

It's my turn, and I get three large scoops of Oreo ice cream topped with sprinkles, chocolate M&Ms, cherries, and hot fudge sauce. I take a seat in the Cave across from Alders and sure enough, the XO makes another pipe.

This time he sounds apologetic as he speaks: "Good evening, *Winnipeg*, it seems we've made such a hit in the news back home that the government of Canada wishes us to extend our time in the Box to get some more good publicity."

He pauses briefly before continuing, "We will not be making port soon. I don't know when we'll be making port next, but once I find out I will let you all know as soon as possible." He pauses again, his voice not unkind, "I just want to tell each and every one of you how proud I am of all your hard work over the past thirty days. I know you will continue to make me proud. That is all."

People groan. There's nothing to do but get up and get a second bowl and bury our frustrations in delicious ice cream.

FEELING THE MOTORS

I walk to the MCR to meet JD for rounds and I see tired faces, downcast gazes, and slumped shoulders. I'm sure I look the part too. JD meets me looking completely depressed. Without a word he signs out the triangle and leaves the MCR. I follow, and he doesn't seem to notice me. He walks quickly; I struggle to keep up. We come to the forward AC plant, and he sighs heavily as he opens the door. Not even bothering to look at me he lifts his arm, points to the motors in the corner and says in a condescending tone, "Get over there."

My gaze follows his pointing. In order to feel those motors I have to climb over a bunch of ducting. I'm suddenly seized with irritation. He's just too tired and lazy to do it himself so he gets me to do it. That's all I do. The work no one else wants to do. JD continues to stand and point.

"What are you waiting for, I said get over there!"

The thought of climbing over ducting right now seems like too much effort for me too, and my apathy and irritation win out. "Get over there yourself!" I hear myself saying, "you're the watchkeeper here, you go feel those motors."

"I'm tired of your attitude!" JD explodes at me, "I'm done doing rounds with you!" He storms off down the flats.

I'm left standing outside the forward AC plant feeling horrible. I'm about to be in more trouble, I think miserably to myself. All because of some lousy ducting. I kick the bulkhead angrily. I don't know what to do now. I wrench open the forward AC plant door and climb furiously over the ducting. I feel the stupid motors in the corner which always feel the same. Why do we even bother feeling the motors? They're all attached to heat sensors anyway. I climb back into the flats and finish rounds by myself.

I walk back into the MCR timidly. I'm expecting to get an earful at any moment. No one reacts. I stand there, and no one even notices that I'm there. I return the triangle and sit at my console, flipping through the screens to check our systems. JD is nowhere to be seen. I feel nervous and decide I had better find a reason to disappear. I spend the rest of the watch doing lamp-ups by myself, dreading the trouble that I know is coming.

That's the last time JD stands watches with me. I don't see him anymore.

Sure enough, the next day Alders comes to find me. "Follow me," she tells me as she leads me to the Cave. Here we go again.

She sits me down at a table in the Cave and explains, "OS Peffers, it's important to feel all the motors during rounds. Usually once the heat sensor is activated, the damage is already done to the motor. This way we catch it early and prevent damage." Alders sounds tired as she continues, "This is an important part of your training as an ETOW. Whenever a watchkeeper tells you to do something it's important that you do what you're told."

I listen, feeling a stifled, trapped irritation. Of course it's not about the motors. The irritation is all about the way people treat me disrespectfully, and there's nothing I can do about it. I listen, but now I'm distracted by Alders' thick, perfectly black, perfectly straight eyelashes. She blinks, and they move through a perfect arc. Her face and eyes are perfect as usual.

I hear her call my name, and my attention returns to the conversation. "OS Peffers, do you understand?"

I hate her, and I hate how I have to respond. I hate the words as I say them: "Yes, Master Seaman."

Speaking of hating things, I start to hate the rumours. They spread quickly about how we'll be making port in five days. Five days comes and goes, and we're still sailing. Rumours spread that we're going to Dubai. Rumours spread, and I quickly start to ignore them. All I know is that I'm very tired and quickly becoming invisible. Except when a man wants to stare at me. Then I'm so very visible that I want to disappear. My focus narrows to one watch at a time. There's no existence after then, and I quickly forget life before then. Four-hour chunks, that's all.

Jed was right about sleep deprivation and accidents. Pellier was doing maintenance in the galley one day, and he neglected to drain the hot water from the equipment. The ship rolled and the door flew open, dumping boiling water down his legs. He ended up with second-degree burns on his thighs. The doc removed him from the watch rotation for a few days. I start to think, if I get injured I can get a few days of rack. I marvel at what I'm willing to go through to get more sleep.

Everyone's so tired that no one talks to me except Jed. Rounds are carried out in heavy silence, and I dutifully feel all the motors. Lamp-ups are carried out in silence too. Whole watches go by, and there's no need for verbal communication between the on watch ET and me.

One day I'm sitting in the chart room with Jed, and he's telling me more stories. "Just you wait…the random face punches in the flats haven't even started yet," he chuckles dryly to himself before going on. "We're all feeling the stress right now. Random acts of violence are just around the corner; the tension is everywhere." Jed pulls out his chocolate-covered coffee beans again and shares them with me. "All it'll take is a wrong look," he warns me.

With mounting stress, we continue to please our government by circling our Box over and over again. The distress calls are unrelenting, but I don't go to the bridge anymore. I mostly just pretend they aren't happening.

I'm on the Afternoon watch with Dale. He leaves the MCR, and I don't know where he went. I'm sitting at my console with my package in front of me, but I'm too tired to focus anymore. I'm still expected to work, so I sit and stare at the page in front of me.

Winnipeg makes a sharp turn and we roll thirty degrees. Objects fall and hit the deck, then there's an alarm. The on-watch stoker reports: "The starboard GT just tripped!"

I find myself laughing as I continue to stare dumbly at my work. We've already lost our PDE and our last standby generator. I start to will *Winnipeg* to break more then. If she breaks enough, surely we'll be forced to make port.

The engineering officer of the watch makes the emergency pipe: "MCR response team, MCR. MCR response team, MCR."

Within seconds the MCR is crawling with stokers and officers. The port GT is started so we aren't drifting, and an investigation is launched. The stokers can't find why the starboard GT tripped. People mutter about gremlins, rubbing their eyes tiredly.

MS Peters, the on-watch stoker, points something out: "A coffee cup fell during the turn, and it might have hit the button on the console that trips the starboard GT."

No other explanation can be found. The EO makes a decision then: "Nothing can be placed on top of the consoles anymore," he tells us.

Our coffee cups are placed on the deck by our chairs. It's not long before someone knocks over their mug, and it's the ODs that are ordered to clean up the spilled coffee.

CESSPOOL

"Good morning, *Winnipeg*," the XO's voice sounds throughout the ship. "Today is day forty straight at sea, for anyone who is counting. We will be making port this afternoon in Karachi, Pakistan." The XO pauses before continuing, "We will only be in port for about eight hours, and it's mostly just to take on more groceries. I'm sorry it's not a longer port visit. That is all."

We've run out of fruits and vegetables, and the cooks are down to serving pasta and meat. We joke about who will be the first to come down with scurvy.

I smell Karachi before I see it. The stench of raw sewage begins to permeate the ship.

I'm sitting with Jed again in the chart room.

"We are, after all, in the sphincter of the world," Jed sighs. "Threats have been made against our task group by terrorist groups in Pakistan, so most of SNMG1 has decided to stay at sea."

The Canadians go in though. Of course that will never make it to the news.

I spend a few hours with Jed in a market close to the jetty. There's no chance of relaxing here. All around us are Pakistani soldiers armed with Chinese AK-47s and the sharp accusatory stares of men. There are no Pakistani women here. The men here stare at me worse than the men on ship.

I spend a few hours storing ship. The veggies look wilted, and the broccoli is crawling with little black insects.

"Fucking ragheads," the OS next to me mutters.

I feel alien here. We're a long way from home. Come evening, I'm standing on the upper decks staring down into the brown sewage cesspool *Winnipeg* is sitting in. She has no choice but to take it in. Sea water is used to cool our machinery, and right now that dirty, brown liquid is flowing through all her sea water circulation pumps and pipes. It's a unique kind of inconvenience to have to see this. A condom floats into view, and I close my eyes. I go back down below and wait for us to leave.

Within the next few days a gastrointestinal illness spreads quickly through the crew. All around me are sickly looking people practically running to the Heads. Frantic pipes are made for on-watch replacements for people who can't leave their stations. In the MCR, people are vomiting into the garbage cans.

I'm in the chart room again with Jed.

"It could get us at any moment," he laughs about the illness that's seizing the crew.

"I know, it's weird I'm not sick…I keep waiting for it to get me."

"The doc suspects it's airborne, but the masses are blaming the food."

"We've all been eating the same thing though, right?"

"Oh, here's a story," Jed leans back in his chair, the bag of chocolate-covered coffee beans already on his desk. He grabs a few, and hands me the bag before continuing. "One of the Sea King pilots got so sick he actually soiled himself while flying!"

I wince while I munch the coffee beans. "Wow, that must have really sucked."

"What can you do? There's no toilet on-board those things."

"Yeah, how embarrassing."

"The guys all had a good laugh about it, including the doc when the poor guy showed up in sick bay after the flight. That's how I heard about it."

Jed stashes the bag of coffee beans back in his filing cabinet.

"The doc is actually busy right now. Some people are so dehydrated that they're in sick bay on saline IVs."

"Really?"

"Yeah. One guy ended up with a heart infection, had to be evacuated by helo to the nearest hospital; the trip's over for him now."

"Wow."

"He's really pissed actually; last I heard, he really wanted that medal."

"He didn't have enough time in the Box?"

"Nope, we need fifty-nine days for the medal."

I groan. Fifty-nine days never seemed so long.

"The doc estimates anywhere from one-half to two-thirds of the crew are sick right now," Jed informs me.

"I'm still waiting," I shrug, wondering if my next meal will be my undoing.

"Same here," Jed agrees. There's a lull in the conversation. "How are you doing with the watches... are you a zombie yet, Peff?"

"I'm getting really, really tired. I snapped at JD...or he snapped at me, I don't know...all I know is we're not doing watches together anymore."

FUCKED

I start to float exhausted through my watches. I'm doing rounds before the Forenoon watch with Pellier. We've split the ship in two, and he's doing the forward half. I drift along the catwalks alone in the aft AMR. I reach automatically for the motors now. It's a choreographed dance carried out mindlessly. The numbness is welcome; it makes the fear seem far away. If *Winnipeg* is going to blow up while I'm down here alone then there's nothing I can do to stop it. The random loud noises seem far away too, and I jump less.

I come back up to three deck and head into the aft switchboard, making my way forward through the ship. PO 2 Perrant is sitting at the laptop here. He sees me and smiles, and I notice how his gaze lingers for just a moment too long. He blushes, going back to his work. I pretend not to notice and continue the automatic ritual of doing rounds. I press the lamp test button and check the boards briefly. The same burnt-out indicating lights are still burnt-out. I move on to the insulation test button.

"How are you doing?" Perrant asks from his desk.

I glance over my shoulder at him, and the eye contact makes him blush again. I look away and tell him, "It's another day in paradise."

He's playing a first person shooter game on the laptop. I have to squeeze past him and check behind the switchboard. We're careful not to look at each other while I do this.

On my way out I ask him, "How are you doing?" while I study my boots.

He sighs heavily and tells me, "I just kill them all." I look up and see he's referring to his game, "I just kill them all."

Stafford shows me how to do bunk light maintenance while I'm Turning-To. The bunk lights on every rack are cheaply made and often break. I'm forced to get up close and personal with other people's racks. There's no avoiding the filth that some people live in. I shudder as I avoid piles of used tissues next to pictures of pin-up girls. I'm forced to get up close and personal with Stafford too. In order to show me how to open the lights up and remove components we squish in so closely that I can smell his deodorant. We laugh awkwardly about it.

Sexual tensions are on the rise throughout the ship. There's a no-scent policy on-board, but the doc is wearing aftershave. One of the male Messes toward the stern has started a masturbation contest. The men are keeping score on the whiteboard.

Meanwhile, in my Mess, I'm getting a shake. It's the most hated of watches, the Morning watch. I wish I were dead as I drag myself out of my rack at 0330. My body runs on muscle memory as I go through my washing routine with my eyelids so heavy my eyes are barely open. I'm so tired I feel dizzy as I make my way to the Cave to grab a cup of coffee before rounds.

The MCR cleaning is under way, and it's back to being split between the watchkeepers. I'm ordered to take out the gash. I head up to the CO's airlock again, taking the long way. I think that maybe fresh air might help to wake me up. I come to a stop on the port boat deck. *Winnipeg* is lit up with silver moonlight. The boat deck is empty except for WO Genette sitting on the bench with her laptop.

She sees me in the moonlight and asks, "Do you ever sleep? I hardly ever see you in your rack."

Wearily, my shoulders slump. "No, that would get in the way of my training."

She looks at me with something like pity and shakes her head, patting the bench next to her. "Have a seat," she says kindly.

I drag the gash over to the bench and slump down heavily.

"Things are slowly changing in the CF," she says. "More and more women are making it into the higher ranks now."

"I don't know a single female chief in my trade. In fact I don't know a single female senior NCO in my trade. No one's made it that far yet."

"What's your trade?"

"Marine electrician."

"It is changing, give it five years. Just hang in for five more years, and you'll notice a real difference."

I think about it; in five years Robertson will be retired. He'll probably be a chief. I look out to sea and see bright, glowing spheres drifting past us in the water: jellyfish. I think they must be beautiful in the moonlight, but I don't feel it.

We're RASing again, and I go to the shop to gather up the winch controller and cable. Robertson is in the shop. He's joking around with Alders, and she's laughing. I notice he keeps touching her. On the shoulder, on the arm. A playful kick on the leg. She smiles and laughs.

Robertson stops me on my way into the flats and drops a pop quiz on me. "Hey, Nick, tell me all the breaker locations for all the winches on-board!" He sounds enthusiastic, like he knows I'll get this. I urge my exhausted mind to recall the required info, but all I get is a blank. I know it's written down, and my hand goes to my pocket.

"No cheating," he tells me. I wasn't aware that checking my notepad was considered cheating. I'm left standing there shaking my head. Nothing. I review my notes every day but I can't recall it now, thinking through a thick haze of fatigue.

Robertson's tone changes to serious. He tells me, "As a qualified RAS ET you should know from memory what I'm asking of you. What if something breaks during the RAS? How will you be able to respond quickly if you're digging around in your notes?"

I want to tell him it wouldn't take more than a few seconds of digging for me to get to the info, but by now I know that's considered talking back so I just stand there mutely.

"I'm going to get one of the guys to do some remedial training with you. You should know this by now."

A far away kind of anger surfaces vaguely through my numbness as I reply with the expected "Yes, PO."

The RAS goes normally, but I am so tired I'm afraid of making mistakes. I focus as intensely as I can and I thankfully do everything right. When it's over I'm exhausted from focusing for so long. I'm supposed to be Turning-To when not on watch, but instead I hide in seven Mess and take a nap on the couch.

On day fifty straight at sea we come alongside in Djibouti. We're only here for two days. Alongside duty watches are assigned, and I have my first DC watchkeeper watch in the MCR in the morning. Tired and overwhelmed, I sit in fear of the massive console in front of me. I hope there will be no emergencies because I know I'll screw up. While alongside the only person who has to stay in the MCR is the DC watchkeeper. I sit briefly at the stoker's console logging the machinery on the hour when Donalds strolls in.

He's drunk and wearing civvie shorts. There's a rule in the MCR that you don't enter this space while drunk, while wearing civilian clothes, or while wearing shorts. He's breaking three rules as he meanders over to sit next to me.

Everyone else in the MCR gets a nervous expression and quietly leaves the compartment. I'm trapped alone with Donalds. He leans in close and asks me quietly, "Are you a virgin?"

My mouth drops open and I stare at him. I just don't know where to start with that one. He sits there gazing at me, waiting.

"Are you!?" I ask finally. What do you say when you can't tell someone how to act?

"No," he tells me. "What are your plans for this foreign port? There's a nice hotel here."

"I'm busy," I blurt out, continuing to fill in the log. Finally Donalds gets up and wanders out.

I get some precious time off, and more than sleep I want to leave the ship. I take an old tour bus with a group of people into the savannah to a cheetah reserve. I team up with Jed, who still keeps his sexual needs to himself. We walk around in the hot sun drinking old-fashioned glass-bottle coke. The silence screams at me after the constant drone of *Winnipeg*'s engines. I find the whole experience of being on land too still and quiet.

After the cheetah reserve, I force myself to explore Djibouti. I've lost interest in seeing new things, but I know this is a once-in-a-lifetime destination for me. I find myself on a bus by myself with no passport but I find I don't really care.

The driver turns around in his seat and smiles at me, saying, "Don't worry, sista, I take good care of you!"

The bus takes me through slums I've never seen before. Mounds of trash stand as tall as buildings, and people wearing colourful kangas sift through it. Emaciated dogs run around sniffing the trash. The bus swerves to avoid a body lying in the gutter. I stare at the dust-covered, limp form lying on the ground, trying to see if he's alive or dead. I finally give up once he's too far away. I guess I'll never know.

I find my way to the one hotel. I walk through marble pillars and exquisitely crafted wood furniture. There was another body in the gutter right next to the hotel. A crisply dressed bellboy hands me a bleached-white towel and opens the door to the outdoor pool for me. I see manicured lawns and flower bushes. I put on my bathing suit and step into warm water. All around me are the ship's company. They're all talking among themselves. I make my way to the edge of the pool over-looking the ocean and sit alone.

Alders comes up to me briefly. "Hello," she says politely.

I smile mechanically at her.

"I was just leaving." She waves goodbye and wades out of the water. I turn away again to watch the ocean.

That evening we're advised to go out in groups. I'm a stranded loner on the flight deck as I watch groups of friends team up and head out. I don't want to, but I make myself try to visit the market. I will record these moments with my camera, and even that feels like a chore. I'm about to give up on ever leaving the boat when a group of stokers comes to stand next to me on the flight deck. Donalds is among them.

"There's room in our group for you," he says.

I consider this and figure there's not much Donalds can do to me while in a group, so I tag along. No one talks to me, and I don't talk to anyone.

In the market, Donalds is the biggest, fattest one in the group. The locals assume he's in charge. All the shopkeepers shout their wares and pull me by the arm, dragging me into their shops.

"Sista, sista, you come, you see, you buy!" they tell me. Donalds keeps a protective watch, over me and quickly grabs me away. The shopkeepers don't argue with fat Donalds. They call him Big Boss, and when I try to buy a mask the shopkeeper tells me I better check with Big Boss first. Big Boss comes over and gives me his consent then goes about bartering the price down for me far lower than I would have gone. I have to concede that Donalds is useful in Africa.

The brief break only makes resuming sailing even harder. We resign ourselves to our watches as we head back out into our Box. Almost instantly tensions run high again. I'm tired of training, tired of sailing, and now I just wish this experience was over. I see the ocean now as a stark, salty waste. It's ugly and flat and featureless. I can't believe I used to think it was beautiful. People were never meant to live out here. You need to surround yourself with technology in order to survive, and it seems like the most unnatural thing in the world. Piece by piece *Winnipeg* is breaking, and our layers of technology are slowly failing.

DAY FIFTY-SEVEN

All it takes is a few days of sailing again and the exhaustion returns ten-fold. The XO gets on the pipe with encouraging news. "Good afternoon, *Winnipeg*, I have some good news. We are only required to be in the Box for nine days this time. Hang in there; we're almost done. That is all."

Hearing this news, I would think that would make the next nine days easier, but instead I start counting and time seems to drag on slower than ever. There are two kinds of sailors: those who count and those who don't count the days spent sailing between ports. I'm naturally a non-counter. I prefer to surrender to the disorientation.

One day I wake up in my rack feeling strange. Something's not right. I check my wristwatch and a jolt of adrenaline shoots through me as I realize I'm an hour late for my watch. Shit! I scramble out of my rack as fast as if bong-bongs were happening. I jump into my uniform, pull on my boots, and button my shirt while I make my way to the MCR. I show up with morning breath and bed-head. The ET console is empty. Donalds sees me and understands what's happened. No one shook me. He tells me kindly that I can always put a shake in with the stokers.

Adrenaline fades, and exhaustion takes over again. I'm so relieved that I'm not in trouble I feel light-headed. I walk forward to the Heads to carry out my washing routine, then I spend the rest of my watch in the MCR trying to keep my eyes open while I sip coffee and stare use-lessly at my training package.

I'm late for my next watch and the next. It seems the ETs have forgotten about me. Not forgotten, I think bitterly. Just haven't bothered. It's been sinking in, the way rounds are carried out in silence. In the way I'm not invited to go out in foreign ports anymore. I'm a burden to them. I showed up needing training. The most training. Holloway and JD are technically just as qualified as me except they both did electronics diplomas before they signed up.

It's such a bother to have to train me, and now I am Outcast. Ignored. Rejected. All I wanted was to fit in, to be one of the guys. I've been working my ass off harder than I've ever worked before in my life. I'm sitting at my console, and I can't stop the tears from falling down my face. I wipe them away with my uniform sleeve. I wonder how many tears my uniform is going to absorb during this sail. It still looks spotless.

As soon as I'm off watch I climb up to the chart room, but as soon as I open the door I see MS McNeil sitting in Jed's seat. She's the junior met tech on-board. I suddenly remember Jed is gone right now. He flew out of Djibouti to use his mid-deployment leave. She asks kindly if she can help me, and I make a show of checking one of the fluorescent lights.

I put a shake in with the stokers, and to my pleasant surprise I find Pellier gently shaking me awake. In the MCR I tell him how the others haven't been shaking me. He's surprised. He tells me he had no idea. Kelvin shows up for rounds and acts surprised to see me up.

"Peff! You made it," he exclaims.

"Don't worry, I'll stay out of your way," I tell him flatly.

Timeless days go by again, and I've broken through to a whole new level of tired. I no longer feel any emotion. For days I am an automaton. I go through my work mechanically. I am just a passive observer. I feel nothing when Robertson tells me to be faster for the steering gear breakdowns. I feel nothing when the hydraulic pipes jump out at me. I stand between the GTs alone in the FER while we're chasing pirates, and the thunder of forty-thousand horsepower shakes my very soul, but I feel nothing.

I'm marveling at this new perception of the world as I fill in another cathodics report when Stafford comes into the shop. He looks pissed. "I've been ordered to give you remedial training. The PO 1 tells me you still haven't memorized the breaker locations for the winches." Stafford sounds angry.

I had been wondering when that was going to come back to haunt me.

"Get off the computer right now!" He stands there impatiently.

In the centre of unfeeling, I log out and start to follow him through the ship. I drift like a ghost. It's night again, and *Winnipeg* is red.

He takes me out onto the fo'c'sle to show me the winches again. I pull out my flashlight to read the brass nameplates and record the info in my notepad again.

"Hurry up!" he tells me as he takes me around the port and starboard winches. I scribble as quickly as I can, and in my exhausted state I have a weird moment while I'm watching my hand write and I feel like it's not my hand doing the writing, but someone else's.

Next he leads me below decks again up forward and starts to show me the power panels again. He's fuming.

"You should know this by now!" His voice is hostile. I suppose he could be in his rack sleeping, but he's been ordered to train me. I am an inconvenience.

"Move faster, let's go!" he yells at me as we head aft to the forward switchboard.

I'm standing outside the switchboard, bathed in red, writing in my notepad when he finally explodes at me. His voice is a forced whisper because it's night outside officers' cabins. He would be yelling, but instead he hisses at me.

"I'm appalled at your training progress! I'm going to have you crawling all over the place so that you learn your lesson! I'll even send you to the Black Deck to do lamp-ups there! I'm going to work you so hard, harder than ever, until you get it right! Because you can't get anything right!"

He takes a breath.

"People are tired of training you! Nobody wants to be on watch with you anymore. What…what are you even doing here? Why are you even here? You don't even belong in the military!"

I'm standing with my pen touching paper. This is when it hits me. You don't even belong in the military. A sudden violent rage consumes me, and I am burning with it. The sudden contrast from the numbness is shocking. It overwhelms my discipline and reason. I look over at him in the red lighting.

He's just touched on my greatest insecurity: the fear that I won't fit into the Navy. I wanted it to be the family I could never seem to find elsewhere, and I've put the better part of half a decade into stubborn, single-minded training. I've been sacrificing everything else in my life for this. My relationship with Roy, who is my only real emotional support, is hanging by a thread.

Thinking about Roy injects a heavy layer of grief into the rage as it builds and sweeps through my mind. Now I am unthinking. All I want to do now is hurt Stafford. I'm folding my notepad and turning to face him now. He's still ranting, but I've stopped listening. I forget military deportment and rank.

"Go fuck yourself!" I turn and walk blindly away.

I'm vaguely aware that Stafford is following me, trying to get my attention. I ignore him and walk the automatic path to my rack. I can't think of anything else to do, anywhere else to go. I can't think at all because of the wall of emotion spilling over my exhausted mind. I quit, I think as I climb into my rack and pull the fire blanket over my head. Heart pounding, sweating, shaking, the anger boils over and turns to deep, ruined sorrow.

My heart pounds long and slow, and I curl up under the blanket from the pain. I can't stop myself and I cry and cry. Alders enters my Mess and opens my curtain.

"Come to the shop, Peff, and tell me what just happened," she sounds tired.

I'm suddenly angry again and I turn to face her.

"Fuck off! Leave me alone, charge me if you have to, I don't care. Just leave me alone!"

I curl up again and pull the blanket back over my head. I hear Alders leave without another word.

Time stretches on, and *Winnipeg* bucks gently. Gradually I calm down and start taking deep breaths. My heart rate returns to normal. Alders comes back into the Mess.

"The PO 1 is waiting for you in the shop. You have ten minutes to meet him there," she says icily and walks out again.

I slowly get down to the deck again. My whole body feels tight. I make my way to the shop, my eyes all red and swollen from crying.

Robertson and Alders are waiting for me. I step out of the deep-red lighting and squint as I step into the glaring white light of the shop. Robertson closes the door and I'm trapped again.

I recount the conversation with Stafford as ordered. Robertson tells me Stafford will be dealt with, but my own actions are now out of his hands. It will be up to the coxn whether or not I face disciplinary action. It's day fifty-seven.

ACCUSED

The next day I'm called to the coxn's office. He hands me a package of paperwork outlining two counts of insubordination brought forward by my chain of command and the date and time for my summary trial. I get even less sleep over the next twenty-four hours as my Div O, Lieutenant (N) Dyssart, meets me (during his waking day working hours of course) while I'm off watch to give me my pretrial counsel.

He sits down with me in the degaussing room. There are no chairs in this small compartment so he sits on the deck and I sit on a hatch. He explains the process of the summary trial and what actions and lines I am to play out and when.

"And here is your speech, OS Peffers. You recite it when the XO prompts you to do so." Dyssart hands me a piece of paper. I glance over it quickly. It reads that I'm to plead guilty and say that I take full responsibility for my actions and that I will endeavor to improve my self-discipline and interpersonal relationships in my shop.

Dyssart pauses while I read, then he regards me.

"Don't cry," he says. "Some people cry. It won't help the court's opinion of you."

I stifle my frustration again. I'm wondering if he'd be giving me this advice if I were a man. I consider my general numbness over the past immeasurable passages of time and decide that crying won't be a problem for me.

Dyssart goes on, "PO 1 Roberston will be your character reference; it sounds like he'll make a good reference for you. He will speak just before you." Dyssart pauses and glances through some sheets of paper he has with him.

"The witnesses will be MS Alders and LS Stafford." He looks up from his papers.

"The coxn will call the drill moves, and the XO will be the presiding officer."

Dyssart puts the pages down on the deck next to him. "Yours won't be the first summary trial on this deployment. In the last two ports, charges were brought up against a few people who were excessively drunk." He looks me in the eye then. "Yours will be the only one for insubordination though. It's a fairly serious charge, and it stays on your permanent record. You won't get advance promoted now, unlike most ordinary seamen. You'll have to serve a full four years before you reach the rank of leading seaman now."

I'm filled with regret over my angry outburst. I think about losing my advance promotion and feel a deep disappointment. I'm still waiting for Stafford to get his punishment. As for the trial, I just want to get it over with. It's been scheduled for the first day *Winnipeg* leaves the Box.

Dyssart chats with me then.

"How is your training going?" His tone of voice is friendly.

"According to my training PO I'm on schedule with my package," I say, trying to inject some emotion into my words. But they come out flat.

"What do you think of all the foreign ports?"

"They're pretty foreign," I shrug. "I took some nice pictures."

It's been a while since someone besides Jed tried to engage me in a real conversation. Underneath the numbness I'm touched.

Dyssart looks thoughtfully at the deck. "You know, it's strange how two hundred and fifty people can all live within four hundred and fifty feet of one another, but we can't seem to communicate."

Some of the numbness melts, I feel a dull ache in my chest.

I may be numb, but my eyes are still sensitive to daylight. I'm sitting on the port missile deck blinking painfully in the sun, and Chelsea climbs up from the boat deck to sit next to me.

"I was in my rack when the conversation between you and Alders happened, and I was just curious...what happened?"

"I was on rounds with Stafford and he totally exploded at me, telling me nobody wants to train me anymore and that I don't even belong in the Navy."

"Wow, you know, Stafford can be a real asshole sometimes. Watch for it in the future."

"He always seemed so nice before that…"

"Yeah, it comes out of nowhere, he just snaps at people." Chelsea pauses then, and we sit together in the sun, watching the ocean waves pass us by. *Winnipeg* sways gently.

"You know," she continues, "it took me almost a year before I felt like I fit in with the crew. *Winnipeg* is a very close-knit group; it's hard to break into."

"I'm noticing that," I sigh.

"You'll find your place in the end; just give it some time."

"Thank you." I am touched by her kind words.

We sit together in silence for a while, then Chelsea goes on: "I have to start rounds soon. See you later, Peff."

Chelsea heads back down the ladder to the boat deck. We're on such drastically different schedules that we basically never see each other. This is the only conversation we have on the deployment.

The day before the trial Cpl Greene, one of the male combat cameras, comes to find me. I'm doing a lamp-up in the wardroom servery.

"Hi, OS Peffers, I need to take your picture." He holds up the professional-looking camera from around his neck.

"Oh, okay, what's the occasion?" I'm screwing a screw back into place on the light fixture.

"You qualify for the Hometowners media event. It's a PR project where people who grew up in small towns get a newspaper picture and article about them serving on-board the now famous pirate hunting HMCS *Winnipeg* for their hometown newspaper."

"I see." I continue to screw in the screw.

"In this case you'll be featured in the…" Greene pulls a pad of paper from his pocket and reads "*Fort McMurray Today.*"

The day before I get punished I am treated like a media star. I try to look natural while I hold my screwdriver just so. In the blinding flash

I see their brief outlines again, arms held high in surrender and those blind, unseeing, desperate eyes.

Winnipeg finishes her time in the Box with no more newsworthy pirate captures. According to the media we successfully captured five pirate vessels during our fifty-nine-day stint. Our mission is defined as a success, and we are heralded as heroes. The Canadian government is haggling with NATO over exactly which medal we qualify for, but we're assured that a medal of some kind is coming our way. We're also assured that the public has taken notice of us, and we are currently "the face of the Canadian Navy." We're even featured in newspaper political cartoons.

THE TRIAL

It's the day of the trial. I'm standing outside the aft section base with Robertson, Alders, and Stafford. My uniform is required to look a step up from everyday work level. My uniform sleeves have been rolled down, and I've had to temporarily remove the utility knife and flashlight from my belt. Thankfully, nobody on ship cares about the condition of my boots. I stand nervously, going over Dyssart's speech in my head. Robertson jokes with Alders. The ceremony starts then, and all three file solemnly into the section base. I am left alone standing at ease in the flats, waiting for the coxn to call me.

I hear my name called out loudly from the compartment, and I slip into the drill.

"Sir!" I respond, snapping to attention. I march into the aft section base and stand in the centre of the room at attention. I stand alone, and all along the bulkheads stand the various people involved in the trial. They form a ring around my peripheral vision. Robertson is standing to my left. The coxn is in the left corner, and directly in front of me, at a podium a few metres away, stands the XO.

While at attention, I can't move a muscle. Except to blink. I am permitted to blink my eyes. It's a disciplined drill move that I mastered in Basic Training. I can't move my eyes. My gaze must fall exactly forward. Usually I find a spot in the centre of my vision and just stare at that spot. In this case, my gaze falls on the XO's shirt collar. I marvel briefly in a detached way about how clean and blue his shirt is. I keep washing mine, but over the past few months a dingy grey residue of diesel smoke has permanently stained my uniform shirts. It marks me for who I am: a member of the engineering department.

I stand at attention. My arms are straight, my shoulders are squared, and my hands form the required shape of a fist down at my sides. My toes are at ninety degrees to my heels. I am conditioned now to clear my mind and listen. Adrenaline is now working to keep me alert through the haze of fatigue. I've been working for twelve hours already today.

The coxn reads the charges and adds a particularly venomous tone of voice (that I didn't have) to the "Go fuck yourself," comment. At his rank he is permitted his interpretations. I'm guilty of two counts of insubordination. The first one for swearing at Stafford, the second for swearing at Alders.

One by one the witnesses are called and they reply with crisp "Yes, sirs" when the coxn asks them if their statements reflect accurately on what happened. In ceremonies the highest rank present is used, so even though the coxn is being addressed (he's normally addressed as 'Swain), there's an officer present so he's addressed as Sir.

Now, the XO orders me to remove my headdress, and in two crisp actions I grab my ball cap with my right hand and pull it down so that it covers my heart. I feel very exposed. Robertson is called to give his character reference of me. I hear him start to speak. He reads from a piece of paper in his hands.

"Ordinary Seaman Peffers is ahead in her training. However, since she has joined the crew in Hawaii she has presented with a constant attitude problem. On her very first day of work as molly she demonstrated a complete lack of respect for and talking back to her superiors…"

Davin is yelling at me "Girl!"

"This ongoing and chronic attitude problem has presented itself in her section base…"

I remember trying to explain to the section base buffer that the bunker gear was dangerously too big for me.

"At her station in the MCR under the engineering officer of the watch…"

I see Donalds telling me again, "Haven't you figured it out yet? You're being punished."

"And in her chain of command under Master Seaman Alders…"

Alder's eyes are piercing into me. They are ice-cold and rimmed in perfect, jet-black mascara and eyeliner.

"Basically everywhere Ordinary Seaman Peffers has worked, she has behaved disrespectfully toward her superiors. She has not made any friends among the department. Ordinary Seaman Peffers is not a team player. During shop meetings she stands in the corner. She doesn't socialize and prefers to spend her time alone. I am personally disappointed in her dismal behaviour since coming aboard, especially after hearing such good things from her instructors. Ordinary Seaman Peffers has failed to live up to the expectations I clearly outlined at the beginning of the sail..."

His harsh words are hitting me like individual slaps in the face, and I struggle to keep up but then suddenly I'm no longer standing in the aft section base. Instead, I'm sitting across from the man in the trailer in Okinawa. His eyes are boring into me, and I'm trapped. He's telling me again that everyone is watching me and that I will have to convince them all that I am worthy. The man's foot is pressing into mine again under the table and his gaze is hungry, so very hungry...

I should have...I am such a fool. Such a fool. I'm consumed with fear. A terrifying, hunted, trapped, helpless fear. I need to get out of here. I'm not safe, I'm not safe. A dizzying confusion fills my head, and I don't know where I am. The room has suddenly gone very cold. Robertson's voice is off in the distance far away, and I can no longer make out what he's saying.

I sense motion in front of me, and I'm back on *Winnipeg* again. There's a face moving, and I'm no longer staring at a shirt collar. The XO moves until he finds my gaze. He puts his own eyes right where I'm staring. I'm looking the XO directly in the eyes. I didn't know I could do that. His eyes are wide and focused intently on me, as if to say it's okay to look him in the eyes now. I look, and I see his eyes are large and brown and soft. There's no hunger or violence here, and the rest of my vision tunnels back outward again and I see the bulkheads and the people in my peripheral vision again.

He holds my gaze then, keeping me present while Robertson finishes his speech. Through this whole ordeal this gaze is the one mercy. Shame washes over me then like heavy waves, and I stare and stare.

I can't feel my body. I don't know how I'm still standing. Gradually, ever so slowly, the XO is nodding his head almost imperceptibly, as if to say yes, you're doing well.

Maintaining his watchful gaze now, he makes a show of dropping his shoulders and a subtle gesture with his chin which tells me he wants me to do the same. I notice my shoulders then, and how they're up around my ears. My whole body returns to me then, and every muscle is clenched tight. I force my shoulders to relax, and they slide back down to a more normal position. The XO watches me carefully and nods a subtle nod of approval.

Robertson's words are finally over, and now the XO makes a subtle show of steadying up. He stands up a little straighter, and his gaze falls somewhere in the distance. Then he returns his eyes to gaze gently at me again and nods subtly. I get the message. Time to return my gaze to staring straight ahead while at attention. He watches me carefully while I drop my gaze back down to his shirt collar.

The XO is speaking now. "OS Peffers, you may now present your side for the court to hear."

Flurries of words are flying through my mind. I think back to my first days on the ship and I wonder how things have gone so wrong. Now I'll never make officer.

The body opens its mouth, and I hear my voice. I'm reciting the speech that Dyssart gave me in degaussing. The words are small, defenceless, condoning. The XO finds my gaze again, and I'm finishing my speech staring into mercy. His large, brown eyes look surprised then and subtly impressed. He thanks me for my input then and begins to write some notes.

I stand forever at attention. I'm gutted. Empty. Shamed. I wait while the higher-ups step into the flats along the starboard corner of the compartment to deliberate and decide my sentence. They emerge quickly. Steel doors creak and scrape. The XO resumes his place at the podium and reads my sentence: "Ordinary Seaman Peffers, I hereby sentence you to five days of punishment duties and a hundred-and-fifty-dollar fine." He puts the paper down on the podium and calls the summary trial to a close. I have been handed the lightest sentence possible. I hear the coxn call my name and call the drill move to dismiss me. The body replaces its ball cap, executes a perfect right turn, and marches toward the flats.

My shin hits the hatch coaming then, and I stumble slightly. Pain brings me back, and I reach out for her then, steadying myself against hard steel. I step over the hatch coaming and I'm walking normally. It's over.

I don't remember walking through the ship. I'm at attention outside the coxn's office and he's telling me to have a seat across from him. He goes over the paperwork and shows me where to sign. This is nothing personal for him, just a business transaction.

He reads from the package of papers about my duties for the five days of punishment.

"While not standing watch you will be mustering outside the forward switchboard, reporting to the petty officer of the watch at regular intervals. The petty officer of the watch will dispense cleaning duties at each of these muster times. Failure to report for a muster timing will result in further disciplinary measures."

The coxn pauses. "Do you understand?"

The body says yes. My hand signs a form, and then he hands me some paperwork he wants me to read over.

I look at the page in front of me and begin to panic. I'm staring at the black lettering. None of it's making any sense. I see the black letters, and I know they form words and those words form sentences, but I can't read. I can tell by the formatting that it's some kind of list. I stare and stare, and I don't know what to do. The coxn is watching me, waiting. Finally I decide my time must be up by now and that should have been enough time for me to read the page. I look up, and he's passing me the pen and pointing to where I need to sign. Numbly, I sign. I have no idea what I just signed for.

"OS Peffers, you are free to go now."

I'm walking down the flats again. Panic is spreading slowly through my mind. I'm at my locker, putting the papers inside. I've forgotten my watch rotation. I'm disoriented. I don't know if I'm going on watch soon. I don't know if the ETOW would care if I showed up. Suddenly all I want is alcohol. Sweet, relaxing alcohol. I need to relax.

On an empty stomach I pick my two beers from the machine, and I see the stokers laughing and joking at their corner table. More than usual, people seem to be staring at me. I head straight to the stoker table and sit down, placing my beers on the table in front of me.

OS Pears tells me, "Don't worry, we won't tell."

"Okay..." I'm confused. Tell what? What do they know? I crack open my beer and swallow it down.

I've been spending time alone because that's what it looks like when I work on my training packages. Finally, tonight, I decide I've trained enough, and now I'm going to talk to these people. They share jokes and stories.

"I was changing the oil on one of the diesel-driven fire pumps on time..." OS Merrit says, "Well I forgot to bleed out the line pressure before I started..." Groans all around the table. Merrit takes a sip of beer.

"I got completely covered in oil!" Laughter erupts from the table then.

"Hey, Peff," OS Ralph, sitting next to me, turns to me now. "Y'ever heard of the pull start?"

I think back to all my training and decide I've never heard of this term.

"No," I say, puzzled. "Is it some kind of procedure?"

"I'll show it to you then," he tells me kindly.

Suddenly he's holding a beer can right next to my ear and cracking it open. It must have been shaken because it sprays me with foam. We all laugh.

I swallow down my second beer and finally the alcohol starts to spread a relaxing warmth throughout my body. I say goodbye and crawl exhausted into my rack still wearing my uniform.

I'M CUTE

The next morning I'm called to the coxn's office again. He sits at his desk with more paperwork in front of him.

"Did you think you were cute, that you would get away with it?" he asks me, irritation in his voice.

All I know is that I'm in trouble again, and I don't even know why this time. My look of confusion only seems to add to his displeasure. He hands me the paperwork then, and demands that I confirm my signature. I can thankfully read again so now I glance over the page. It's the thing I signed yesterday. It outlines all the privileges that have been revoked while I'm under punishment. I read it now for the first time, and at the top of the list it says I may only visit the Cave during mealtimes for the purpose of eating and that any other time for socializing is not permitted. It continues to state that I am not permitted to consume alcohol. Suddenly it all makes sense. All the weird stares, OS Pears' comment about not telling. Someone told.

I'm obviously guilty. What can I say? I don't think the coxn will believe me if I tell the truth.

"Yes, 'Swain, that is my signature." I look him straight in the eyes. "I take full responsibility for my actions."

The coxn seems more satisfied now. "Thank you, OS Peffers, you may go." And he goes back to his writing.

I climb up to the bridge after my watch is over and lean heavily on my pole. The officer of the watch tells me we're en route now to Salalah, Oman. It's a quick trip, and we should be coming alongside tonight. This is our first port since the Box that will actually give us some R&R. Reservations are already being made in the ship's office for the few hotels in the area. I put my name down for one night. This will be my first hotel of the sail. The nice thing about not being molly is more free time in foreign ports.

It was decided in the trial that my punishment duties won't start until after we're under way from Salalah, otherwise I would be confined to ship for the whole port. This is another show of leniency given to me by the XO. I'm still considered to be under punishment since the trial ended, so the Cave is out of bounds. I don't really care since I was never in the habit of socializing there anyway. I'm going to miss the alcohol though. I can't get good sleep without it.

SHOULD'A FUCKED HIM

I've given up trying to do work on my package while not on watch. I've stopped working out. When I'm not doing rounds or wandering through the ship fixing the damn ballasts I'm in my rack. I went down to the ship's laundry during the Mids when no one was looking and stole a pile of fire blankets. Now I sit in my rack propped up against the bulkhead and burrow into a thick mound of soft blankets in the deep-red glow. I watch movies on my laptop or listen to soft music and close my eyes. I'm too exhausted to read for pleasure.

Time passes in a weird void, and suddenly we're alongside in Salalah. I try to remember the past few days, and I just can't. Jed meets the ship on the jetty, and we make plans to hang out.

The hotel is a palace. Marble pillars and sweeping tapestries. Everyone in this port wears flowing white robes and turbans. People look pristinely clean with bleached-white clothing yet everyone smells like perfume over sweat.

I check in, and I'm told the hotel overbooked and my room is no longer available. In order to make it up to me, I've been upgraded to one of the penthouse suites. I stand in awe at my four-poster, king-size bed, intricately patterned rugs, large antique bathtub, and extra-large balcony overlooking a sandy beach and brilliant blue ocean. I sip a bottle of whisky while I luxuriate in a hot bath. By the time I crawl out I'm so physically drained I barely have the strength to stagger over to the bed. I collapse on the soft mattress, and I'm instantly asleep.

I sleep until the afternoon, then Jed shows up at my door with more whisky. We sit on my large balcony drinking and chatting. I fill him in about Stafford and the trial and he snorts sarcastically, "Your PO 1 really boned you." He sips straight from the bottle, and then hands it back to me. "If an altercation like that had happened in my department I would have settled it inside the department. I assure you, you must have really pissed Robertson off for him to go through all the trouble of the paper-work required to press charges."

I decide to start telling him about some of the other stuff. I explain what happened in Okinawa, and Jed replies with a quick "Yep...you should'a fucked him. Who knows, maybe that guy could have been 'your friend in high places.'"

Afternoon turns to evening, and we order room service. I listen while Jed regales me with war stories. It's evening, and the stars are out.

There's an easy lull between us then, and Jed shakes his head and tells me, "You should have joined the Air Force instead. You're keen, you want the training, you're smart. In the engineering trades in the Navy, people like you just intimidate superiors. They're still a bunch of sexist dinosaurs. They beat the initiative out of young ordinary seamen," Jed sighs. "I've been watching it for years."

In this port I manage to spend three whole days not working. My circadian rhythm begins to even out as I sleep only at night. Three days does wonders, and when we slip I feel somewhat rested. This new-found rest brings back the terror from before about the machinery spaces, and I'm once again jumping at every loud noise.

BIRDS

Over the next five days I'm so busy with punishment duties that I only get two to three hours of sleep a day. The rest I got in Salalah is quickly wiped away, replaced with more exhaustion. I am on BIRDS (Boys In Real Deep Shit). Of course officially the Canadian Forces is opposed to sexual harassment, and so punishment was renamed PUP (Personnel Under Punishment). Everybody still refers to it as BIRDS, though.

I'm required to present myself for inspection to the petty officer of the watch every few hours while not on watch. Alders orders me to do all the cleaning for the entire department every day, which is technically a form of double jeopardy because my punishment should only be managed through the coxn's office now. I'm so busy scrubbing decks when not doing rounds or on watch that the coxn notices I'm hardly meeting any of my muster timings. I have a brief moment of hope when the coxn comes to the shop to tell Robertson to make me more available for my muster timings, but nothing further comes from that request.

Now, when I'm not doing rounds or on watch or cleaning the ET spaces, I'm scrubbing Heads for the petty officer of the watch. I think I've scrubbed all the Heads on-board by the time my five days are up. The time passes quickly because I'm so busy. I work and sleep and repeat.

Standing for inspection is a pleasant experience. The petty officer of the watch looks me over and checks my dress. The act of someone studying me for a few seconds makes me feel less invisible. He's unusually pleased with my appearance and tells me so.

The rumour mill spreads news of my insubordination throughout the crew. If anyone didn't know who I was before, they now know me as the Insubordinate OD. Every senior NCO now makes it their personal mission to watch me like a hawk for the slightest attitude problem.

Just before I'm done doing BIRDS, Robertson comes to find me and takes me to the shop. He closes the door, and I'm trapped alone with him. My heart starts pounding in my chest.

"OS Peffers, I've been doing some thinking and I've decided to institute an additional remedial measure. Every two weeks now for the next three months you will report to me and the baby EO in the aft switchboard for feedback sessions. This will give me some time to counsel you on your behaviour."

Robertson pauses while I stare at the deck, starting to sweat.

"I assure you, this will help," Robertson goes on. "We're almost at the halfway mark in the sail, so the feedback sessions should wrap up just before we return home."

He hands me more paperwork to sign saying that I'm under more disciplinary measures now. I stand there staring at the buffalo in the ship's crest on his uniform jacket. The embroidered buffalo looks sad, with his head downcast.

"OS Peffers, I need you to look me in the eyes so that I know you understand what I've just told you."

I hate him as I comply, and I don't ever want to see his eyes again.

I'm doing rounds with Stafford, and he looks over his shoulder at me in the dark-red lighting. "It's been a few days since I went above deck," he says, and he leads me up into the hangar and out onto the flight deck. I'm exhausted, and suddenly I'm staring up at a beautiful night sky.

All the pressure of people crammed in like cattle releases slightly then, and I find I'm crying silently, my face turned upward at the stars. I'm suddenly overcome with a strong, piercing regret. How did I get so turned around? I remember her then, before I got to know her, next to the jetty in Hawaii with the sun blazing behind her. The red of the Canadian flag was lit up like fire. I was so optimistic. The last thing I wanted was to get in trouble. Stafford goes to stand away from me in the darkness, over by the guardrail.

I'm standing in the airlock of the aft AMR and I pause, looking back at Stafford. I'm not angry at him anymore. "You know I don't have a problem working with you, right?"

Stafford looks at me briefly then replies softly, "Yeah, I know."

BIRDS is finally over, and I have some free time again. It's night, and I take my iPod and walk to the very end of the boat. I stand on the quarterdeck and lean heavily on the guardrail, staring down at the churning waters. The helo is out on the flight deck lit up with floodlights, and the air det crawls over the fuselage doing maintenance. The light from the floodlights reflects on the water.

For the first time in months we have waves again. The Gulf of Aden was just a flat, calm pool; now, finally, I see waves rearing up in the restless dark waters. I stand there for hours, and people give me a wide berth. People meet friends and sit and smoke, but they are sure to do it well away from me.

THE EO WANTS TO TALK TO ME

I'm just starting the Forenoon watch. Rounds are done, and it's 0800. The day workers are just getting up, the red lighting is switched to white, and the flats are once again filled with people. I stop in at the shop on my way to the MCR, and PO 2 Perrant gets my attention.

The shop is crowded as usual and I press in to see what Perrant wants. He looks very serious. I have a sinking feeling before he even starts to talk.

"OS Peffers, the EO wants to talk to you." His tone of voice is serious.

The EO is just below the XO in the chain of command—way, way above me. I've already been told by Perrant that if an officer wants to talk to you it's usually never a good thing. For an OD it usually means one thing: I'm in trouble. And this is a very high-ranking officer (from the perspective of a ship) so it must be big trouble that I'm in.

"I don't know what it's about. I was just told to present you to the EO," Perrant tells me.

Kelvin and JD mock me with, "Oh Peff is in trouble again!" I feel anxious and smile nervously at their words.

Perrant leads me up a series of ladders and along a few flats until we're outside a cabin on two deck. I follow behind him, feeling like a schoolchild being escorted to the principal's office. What have I done this time? And for it to go as high as the EO...

"Wait here," Perrant tells me in a hushed tone as he knocks politely on the cabin door. I'm standing with my back to the bulkhead staring at a white bulkhead in front of me, feeling a mixture of curiosity and fear.

The door opens, and a brief exchange of words follows: "I've brought you Ordinary Seaman Peffers."

"Thank you, please bring her in."

"Ordinary Seaman Peffers, the EO will see you now." Standing in the doorway, Perrant gestures to the EO, and the EO gestures to inside his cabin. I follow the gestures like a herded sheep.

It's a normal, everyday cabin: two bunks, a desk, a sink, and mirror. The bunks are stowed, and two chairs are laid out. I stand awkwardly in the centre of the room while the EO closes his door. I'm trapped, and we're alone together. My palms start sweating. I really hope he can't tell about the secret crush on him that I've been harbouring ever since we started doing engineering drills at the beginning of the sail.

He smiles at me. "Please sit," he gestures to one of the chairs and sits down on the other. I take my seat. He faces me, leans forward, gives me eye contact, and says, "The first thing I want you to know is..."

My heart flutters in my chest. This is it, I've done something horrible. I brace myself, returning his gaze.

"That you're not in any kind of trouble." He finishes his sentence and watches me to see it sink in.

It sinks in with relief. "Oh," I say. My voice sounds small. He continues to watch me.

"I just want to check in with you to see how things are going for you."

My gaze wanders to save me from looking him in the eyes. To his left on the bulkhead by the door is something that makes me freeze. Two photographs of cats. Both cats are stretched out on their backs exposing their bellies, looking relaxed and happy. Trust. That's how cats show it. They expose their vulnerable undersides. There's a pain starting in the centre of my chest again.

I'm staring at those pictures, and I'm unable to stop myself. My eyes drink them in. There are so few reminders on ship about the other lives we live when we're not sailing. I haven't seen many other photographs, and the personal touch it lends to this cabin is huge.

I'm vaguely aware that the EO has seen what I'm looking at. He leans back in his chair to give me a better view then turns to his desk, arranging file folders.

Two happy cats are smiling at me lazily. My heart aches, and I still can't look away. The EO speaks again, this time his voice is ever so gentle, "I just want to make sure that you're okay."

I'm confused. No one talks to me like that. Especially not in that tone of voice. What does he mean, am I okay? I look at him.

"Of course I'm okay," I say pleasantly. "My training is going well."

"I'm not worried about that," he tells me, studying me again, "I just want to make sure that you are okay."

I just sort of stop. I sit mutely. My lips, tongue, and throat won't move. There's a wall of anxiety closing in on me fast. No! I'm screaming in my head. Of course I'm not okay. And he's sitting there so compassionately that I just want to tell him everything. I think he would listen. I think he would care. I want to tell him something serious has happened. I want to tell him about Donalds. About Davin. About Okinawa...

I blink. It's basically all I can do.

"Are you okay?" He's studying me again with his eyes.

The wall of anxiety turns into a wave, and the wave freezes solid. There's too much. I can't even begin. And then I feel like if I begin talking I'll end up sobbing my eyes out in front of the EO, and that would be humiliating and then I might get sent home. And I still want to finish the damn sail. Not to mention what might happen once Robertson finds out. He won't be happy, and he has so much power over me.

I swallow and speak, "I'm fine." For good measure, the corners of my mouth curve upward into a smile. I shrug lightly.

The EO gets a pained expression on his handsome face, and he nods and says "Okay," as if he's just received bad news.

"You can come and talk to me anytime," he tells me heavily. The pain in my chest contracts a little. I want to very badly, but I know I probably won't. I'm protecting my chain of command and the people I directly work for because their assessment of me is all that matters. Because that's what the rest of the ordinary seamen do. Because that's what's expected of me.

There's a strange disjointed feeling like I'm not sure how much time has passed, then the EO is smiling and standing. That's my cue so I stand up. He opens his door, and I'm free. I'm out in the flats again, walking back down to the MCR.

Over the next few days I have plenty of time to think about what the EO said to me. I can go talk to him anytime. It sounds like a special privilege. Can I really just walk up to him? Normal military etiquette tells me I need to put in a request, usually a written memo, to my supervisor who would pass it up to the PO 1 who would pass it up to my Div O who would then give it to the EO. That would be normal procedure if I wanted to talk to the EO. But there's no practical reason an ordinary seaman would ever need to talk to the EO, so while the request would go up my chain there's a good chance it would be denied at the lowest level. My supervisor or the PO 1 would tell me I can talk to them instead. I'm sure there would be a patronizing comment about how busy the EO is as well.

But now I have his permission to just go straight to him. It's a special kind of agony, being undecided for a few days. Maybe I should just tell him everything. But I can't risk falling apart now. One day after working for about twelve hours straight, I'm so tired I almost cave in. I even start walking toward his cabin. Fuck it, I'm going to do it, I think. But my body freezes midstride, and then I'm just standing stock still in the middle of the flats. It's like there's an invisible wall in front of me. I just can't go any further. I am Fort Knox. A cold, shaky feeling settles over me as I turn around and head back to three deck.

FRESH WATER PUMP #2

I'm intimately acquainted with most of the pumps and motors on ship now. I know normal temperatures for each, normal sounds, and even normal smells. I've repeated the exact same set of actions going from compartment to compartment, motor to motor, from stern to bow for every watch for the past two months now, and my muscles have every move, every step memorized. I reach out and touch them with the back of my hand.

I think I'm developing a crush on fresh water pump #2. I've started lingering for a few minutes down in the laundry flats where it's found. It's a relatively empty part of the ship. The only traffic is people on their way to the laundry room, people working in the ship's laundry and roundsmen.

During rounds with Pellier I treat it no differently than any other pump on-board, giving it a brief feel with the back of my hand for a few seconds then moving on. I make a mental note though. Once I'm off watch, I'm drawn back to it like an iron filing to a magnet.

It started with a realization. This pump has the best temperature to warm my hands on. Not too hot, like the lube oil pumps down in the forward engine room. Not too cold, like some parts of the fridge compressor. Just right, and the area isn't too noisy. And now there's no one hurrying me along, trying to get a coffee break in before watch.

It has to be fresh water pump #2, which coincidentally is the one we're constantly using. Fresh water pump #1 is located in and behind #2, crammed in a corner next to the opposite bulkhead with an array of pipes running over it. Fresh water pump #1 is not accessible.

So one day I just sort of pause while my hands are touching the pump. It's a grey-painted, cylindrical thing sprouting out of some pipes along the deck. It comes up to my waist. It vibrates gently and radiates such a comforting warmth. It's part of the system that gives us hot tap water. I look around to make sure I'm alone, then I just sort of keep touching it. I spread my palms flat against its smooth, finned sides and lean my legs into it so that I'm resting my weight on it. I'm hugging fresh water pump #2.

At first it feels really awkward, and I'm afraid someone will come down the ladder directly behind me and catch me in the act. What would they think? Has anyone else ever done this? Would they report me once again to my chain of command for inappropriate behaviour? Would they spread more rumours throughout the ship? Would I become even more alienated? Would all this just feed my crush on an inanimate metal object?

After the first few times it gets less awkward and more enjoyable. Now I pause to touch and hug the pump for a few minutes at a time. My cold fingers warm up. My tight muscles relax a little bit. Fresh water pump #2 doesn't judge or intimidate me. It doesn't want anything from me. It doesn't order me to do anything. Best of all, it doesn't want to have sex with me. I can get close to it without fear. It gives me its warmth and asks nothing in return. I can leave it alone in between watches, or if I happen to be unlucky and there's someone else in the compartment. Fresh water pump #2 understands my need for secrecy and doesn't get jealous or lonely; it just waits patiently for my return.

I close my eyes and focus on the warmth in my hands and thighs. I feel the solid warm weight of the ship supporting me while the deck sways gently. I want to stay like this, down here on four deck, attached to a pump. Make me a length of pipe or a bolt in the ship's frame. Make me something as unfeeling and as hard as steel.

Fresh water pump #2 is running hot. A circle has been drawn on its side in black grease pencil and a sheet of paper taped to its top with a table showing temperatures logged every four hours by the ETOW roundsmen. Every set of rounds now I take the laser thermometer with me and point it at the circle on the pump and record the results.

After all it has done for me, I feel real concern for fresh water pump #2. Days go by, and it's kept in service. No repairs are done, and the temperature log fills up fast. Now during my visits it's just a little too hot for my hands. I still touch it as much as I can, but I have to hold my hands a few centimetres away for a few seconds now and then to avoid scalding my flesh. It comes up occasionally in conversation in the MCR, but nobody knows why this pump is running hot.

Robertson tells us during a morning meeting to stop monitoring fresh water pump #2. The piece of paper taped to it is put in the recycling, the grease pencil circle is wiped off. The pump looks normal again, except it's running hot. Robertson tells us it's not hot enough to cause any damage. There's no paint blistering or burning coming from it. Life goes on in the ship, and people's attention shifts to all the other things that are broken on-board.

Now when I visit fresh water pump #2 my heart sinks as my fingers start to burn. I can't get as close to it anymore. I can't lean on it, and I can't touch it for as long as I want. I am shunned, thwarted, pushed away. My sensitive flesh reminds me that I'm human, with narrow temperature tolerances and inconvenient emotional needs. Disappointed and lonely, I withdraw my fingers from the hot metal and head back up to three deck.

UGLY LIKE ME

I continue to hide out in my rack under a mound of blankets. When I listen to music now it just makes me cry. My numbness disappears when I'm in the machinery spaces a tight terror grips me when I'm alone.

I head through the airlock and down the ladder to the forward AMR, and I'm greeted by the sound of music. A rock ballad plays out of a stereo wedged into a corner of the compartment. The song sings of being outcast and watching from a distance, seeing things how they really are, and seeing them dirty.

The space is filled with stokers. They've gutted one of the four large generators and now they huddle in around the machinery, working together to the music.

I relax instantly. It's good to be not alone down here. Add some music, and it becomes a pleasant experience. A stab of loneliness strikes me when I see the stokers working so closely together. It's a team effort for them. So much of my work is done alone. I've never seen the ETs band together like this to get a job done. The master seaman stoker is deep inside the machinery, pointing out various pieces to the leading seamen who nod and ask questions. The ODs stand by with tools and flashlights. Everything on ship is treated as a learning experience, especially when things break.

I pause and take in the scene. Grease-covered machinery parts lay strewn around the catwalks, and there's a gaping black hole in the middle of the generator. I can see straight through what is normally a dense package of machinery parts.

The stokers sweat while they work, oblivious of my presence. Their blue uniform shirts and flushed faces are stained with black grease. Together, they've dismantled fully one quarter of *Winnipeg*'s power generation capability. I can see the guts deep inside her. Inside she's ugly. The black carbon and grease is thick upon metal parts reflecting the golden glow of their portable lights. These diesel generators are designed to be run all out, but they never are. At most they'll be working at seventy-five per cent of their full load so that a margin of reserve power can always be available. The result is incomplete combustion.

Add to the equation all the piping and hoses that bend and flex and a host of leaking water coolers and fuel lines. Fluids drip from her blackened insides into the sump at the bottom of the generators, setting off alarms so often that they mostly are ignored. It's a normal part of rounds to drain out the DGs. A soupy black liquid oozes from the drain and mixes with the greasy bilge water sloshing around under the catwalks.

Everyone in the engineering department agrees that the generators are the weakest part of the CPF design. It's considered completely normal to sail with only half your power plant operational. Unfortunately, rumours of the mid-life upgrades that are being planned in the next few years tell of no changes being made to the generators.

The engineering department toils in obscurity. It's part of the engineering culture down on five deck. Working seamlessly in the background is the preferred way to run the department. There's a sense of pride in a job well done if the bridge never has to pay attention to the engineering side of things. Most of the ship's staff don't pay any attention to the guts of the ship until something essential breaks.

There's nothing more basic and essential to a warship than electric power. The fanciest weapons systems and sensors in the world become useless in the face of a blackout, where all four generators stop working and the ship loses all power. Every other department on-board operates because they get power from the generators.

I watch as a few stokers insert a long metal rod into a large rotating cog deep inside the generator enclosure. They're turning the engine over manually. This is the real *Winnipeg*, I think. I can see the guts of the beast. Dirty, overworked, half-broken, and constantly patched up. I stand invisible in the corner and feel as dirty and broken as the generator.

HALFWAY THERE

More and more I don't remember the days as they go by. Jed had warned me that I wouldn't remember most of it. Maybe it's the mind-numbing monotony of doing the exact same thing every single day. Maybe it's the exhaustion. Whatever it is, life happens in brief disjointed moments now.

I've stopped visiting the bridge. I no longer care about who we're sailing with or what exercise we're doing. It doesn't matter to me in my small ordinary seaman world, and nobody expects me to care. I'm a darkness-loving troglodyte that lives in red night lighting. I learn about where we're going from Jed in the chart room.

I sit sipping warm green tea, sitting on the chart table.

"We're headed to Seychelles now," Jed tells me from his desk. We're both munching on chocolate-covered coffee beans, although the bag is almost empty now.

"I get to take my mid-deployment leave out of there."

"Visiting your boyfriend? Edmonton, right?"

"Yeah."

"Looking forward to it?"

"Absolutely."

"Well, you've only got a few weeks to go."

"Yeah." I think about seeing Roy again, and it hurts so much I push the thought away.

Life drags on, and one day the cooks bake a birthday cake for Dale. The entire department including the baby EO squeeze into the shop and laugh and chat while slices of green cake with blue icing are distributed. True to my reputation but not really caring, I sit in the corner. No one talks to me, and I don't talk to anyone. I try to eat the cake but it's so sweet it makes me feel sick.

I'm doing rounds in the forward AMR when the wakey-wakey song comes on. Today is special, and the XO has a special announcement before it plays: "Good morning, *Winnipeg*. Today is a special day. We are officially halfway there!"

There's a brief pause, then music begins to blast through the speakers. Bon Jovi's "Livin' On a Prayer" fills the space, and I smile. "Take my hand, we'll make it I swear," Bon Jovi assures me. Nobody touches me anymore. I long for someone to take my hand and tell me, "We'll make it I swear." I reach out and feel *Winnipeg*'s auxiliary sea water circulation pump #1. The metal is perfectly warm.

Through it all, the XO's wakey-wakey songs and Jed's weather reports have cheered me up every day. I cling to these moments now. Cpl Slater's snide morning show petered out as soon as morale took a dip during the Box.

I walk into the MCR and find the baby EO, Sub-Lieutenant Finley, sitting at my console reading a book titled *Teach Yourself Electronics*. I don't know what to make of this. I'm on watch with Pellier for the Forenoon watch. He comes up to me looking tired as usual, and tells me he'll be in the shop doing work at the computer. I'm left standing awkwardly next to my console. Finley doesn't seem to notice me, and she continues to read. Due to the rigid hierarchy on-board, she outranks everyone in the room even though she looks younger than me. Fresh out of her engineering degree no doubt. I can't tell her to give me my console back, so I sit in the chair next to her.

I am instantly suspicious. She's sitting in my spot, and she's reading an electronics book. Is this some kind of plan from the higher-ups to get to know me better? Is she here to spy on me and report to the EO? I never seem to get used to the idea of someone watching me, and a new wave of self-consciousness washes over me. Robertson comes to find me and takes me to the shop. He closes the door, and I'm trapped again. My heart starts pounding, and I stare nervously at the deck.

"OS Peffers, I have a new job for you," he tells me matter-of-factly.

Internally, I sigh because I'm not in trouble again. Outwardly I am a mask.

"It is now your responsibility to reorganize the ET library in degaussing." Robertson leans against the counter and crosses his arms. "Over the years, countless amendments have been added to the technical manual binders, and now they're out of order. It will be your job to go through them one by one and make sure they're all in alphabetical order. I expect you to get started on this right away when Turning-To, now that most of your packages are done."

I stand with my eyes downcast, "Yes, PO."

"Just to remind you, OS Peffers, your first feedback session will be just before we reach Seychelles."

"Yes, PO," and with that my heart sinks a little.

I'm sitting on the deck in the degaussing room which houses the ET library. I start at the beginning of the shelves and begin to look through the binders. I notice sections aren't in order, and I begin re-arranging things. It's tedious, lonely, boring work, and I'm sure Robertson knows it. A deep bitterness is filling me as the afternoon wears on and I work at this monotonous, thankless job. I'll be here for weeks I figure as I gauge my progress.

I sneak my iPod into my uniform pocket, and now I listen to music while I sort the library. I'm stuck on a song, Metallica's "The Unforgiven." It's my anthem now, and I play it over and over again.

The watches cycle endlessly, and Finley continues to hang around the MCR for my watches. Donalds is on his best behaviour in the presence of the ma'am and engages her in polite chat. I'm finished with all the parts of my training packages that I can do while the ship is sailing, and I eagerly look forward to the time when I too can chat or browse through a magazine while on watch. Donalds unceremoniously tells me that if I can't work on my package then I have to read the technical manuals. I'm still double-banked so I have to work. No one talks to me, and I don't talk to anyone.

It's the Mids, and I'm so tired I can't read anymore. I have one more long hour to get through before I can sleep. I sit at my console staring miserably at a thick manual explaining the operation of the switchboards. I stare at the page and will the time to pass. Finley is sitting on one of the chairs next to the stoker's console, and she's filling in a log. Her pretty brow furrows, and she runs an embarrassed hand through her long, blond ponytail. She informs Donalds that she just filled in the log incorrectly. Donalds tells her it's okay and to simply start a new page. I stare bitterly at my manual. According to Donalds, Finley can do nothing wrong. Somehow, I think that if it had been me making the log entry mistake I would be getting an earful.

Some chairs have been brought into the aft switchboard; I sit farthest from the door. In front of me in the narrow space are Robertson and Finley. Perrant stands innocuously in the corner. My first feedback session starts, and I have to sit and listen while Robertson talks again. He's come up with a long list of things that I need to improve since the trial. "OS Peffers, you are required to report to your shop master seaman, who is MS Alders, at any time when you get frustrated or angry with anyone and you feel you can't control your temper." Robertson cocks his head to the side before continuing. "I will remind you again that it is your duty to behave in a professional manner and to show respect at all times. You will address all your superiors by their appropriate rank, and you must refrain from swearing when addressing them." He pauses then; I sit like a stone. "You are required to follow all of this advice in order to overcome your deficiency. I will remind you again that failure to overcome this behaviour deficiency of yours will result in further disciplinary actions."

Finley nods in agreement.

I sit there privately fuming but silent. My silence is proper behaviour expected of an ordinary seaman. Next I'm made to sign a printed copy of the feedback session to acknowledge that I have received the feedback. Finley sits there all the while looking pretty and innocent. She has no idea what's really going on.

More days go by. I'm walking down the flats one afternoon, and I hear haunting piano music coming from the stokers' workshop. It snags me, and I'm drawn in. I peek inside, and the compartment is empty of people. I step in and check around. It is quite empty. Someone has left their iPod playing on the bench. The song is "Colorblind" by Counting Crows. I spend a few minutes then listening to the song. A raw voice sings of loneliness and longing. *Winnipeg* moves gently beneath me, and I lean heavily against the counter. A heaviness is weighing me down as I relax, and once the song ends I walk back out into the flats feeling weak in the knees.

LOAD SHEDDING

Winnipeg comes alongside in Seychelles, and we're piped secure. Large tubs of beer on ice are brought down to the aft AMR, and the engineering department has what they call an aft AMR party. All the stokers, hull techs, and ETs, along with all the officers crowd into the aft AMR. People sit on the catwalks and on top of the generators dangling their feet over the edges. It's crowded, and the space is filled with talk and laughter. No one talks to me as I pick up a can of beer and start to drink.

I wander over to the corner where all the ETs have gathered, and JD starts to list all the problems with how Robertson is treating me.

"Having a different ETOW every watch just serves to confuse you, Peff, because everyone has a different approach to training."

I sigh heavily, nodding my head.

"But it's what the PO 1 wants…" Dale says in a resigned tone of voice.

"At least we're getting more sleep, doing one-in-three, six-on-twelve-off," Stafford adds.

Jealous of the other ETOWs' new watch schedule, I say nothing. I think bitterly that it must be nice to get twelve hours off between each watch. I'm still doing one-in-four Turning-To.

"So long as the PO 1 doesn't find out," Alders warns.

Morale seems to be climbing among the ETOWs now; they've even gone back to shaking me.

I wander around some more and numbly observe the various conversations. I'm scanning with my eyes, briefly sharing a look with OS Linden when I'm suddenly grabbed around my lower right hip.

OS Linden looks quickly away from me and suddenly I'm squished into Donalds armpit. I look quickly over at him, and I hear him ask me, "How you doin'?" Anger and disgust flare in me, I push him away roughly. He looks at me and tells me, "You need to learn to relax." I stand there, my skin crawling. All around me the conversations swirl, and it's like I'm invisible again.

Through the crowd I find Alders laughing with some friends, and I tell her that Donalds just groped me. She stares icily at me then, and asks me coolly, "What did you do about it?"

I reply with, "I'm telling my supervisor." What else can I do?

She stares at me with such a hardness and simply repeats herself, "What did you do about it?"

I stare back for a moment. This is how it's going to be. Alders won't help me. She goes back to her conversation, and I'm left standing in the middle of the crowded aft AMR feeling utterly helpless. I quickly climb the ladder and leave the space.

Later in the day we have a brief awards ceremony on the flight deck. Various operators are given plaques for performing their jobs correctly while the entire engineering department looks on unrecognized and ignored. Lonsdale gets an award for shooting his warning shots. He thinks he's hot shit now, but I still remember him hunched over a beer shaking like a leaf.

Minister of National Defence Peter MacKay flies in to personally shake our hands after our publicity in the Box. Cool khakis and a firm handshake with an earnest-sounding "Thank you."

I wander briefly around Seychelles admiring the lush tropical forest. This port feels like a cross between Hawaii and Africa. The next day I board a plane, and I'm carried halfway around the world, back to Edmonton.

Roy hugs me at the airport, but I barely feel it. I'm home again, except it feels unfamiliar now I've been gone for so long. We have sex, and my body moves mechanically. I act out a passion I just don't feel. This is it: two people can't get much closer than this, and yet I feel half a world away. I orgasm, and even my moment of pleasure is tainted. In a brief flash I remember the extreme tension just after the warning shots. I had been so eager to kill then, and now I'm shocked. Oh, how I wanted to kill them. What does that make me? Am I a bad person? I'm overwhelmed with guilt and confusion and, without warning, I burst into tears. Roy is confused and bewildered.

Roy works during the day, and I sleep. I hoard sleep now as if I'll never get enough again. We try to connect, but everything feels awkward. We go for walks in silence and watch movies in silence. I try to talk, I try to reach out, to communicate, but I'm speechless. I don't know what to say or where to start. There's just been too much. Too much has happened. Just as much as I want to connect, Roy stays silent. He seems to draw inward more and more. One day he comes home from work and tells me he no longer knows when he can move out to the Island.

I sit there numbly, comprehension slowly spreading through me. Something inside me is dying until finally there's nothing left. I break up with him then. It's a strange, hollow relief to be walking away from him one last time at the airport. The pain threatens to crush my chest and the tears flow down my face as I walk through security. It's over. We were together for five years.

I drink through the plane rides that carry me back to my current home, the place I wanted so much to belong to. But I've managed to mess that up too. I face more punishment now on *Winnipeg*, which is in Brisbane, Australia. I'm glad to see her again as I walk across the brow and make my way down familiar flats toward my Mess.

THE COXN'S PUNISHMENT

The Aussies love us. Pallets of beer are stacked up on our jetty as a welcome gift. We spend a few days here with the Royal Australian Navy and are invited to use the facilities on the base, including dorms and meals. I spend the entire port nursing a low-grade level of drunkenness. Cute hopping critters called wallabies jump around the base.

We slip with some Australian ships and sail in formation on our way to Melbourne. The first morning spent sailing, the wakey-wakey song is Men at Work's "Down Under." We brave the Tasman Sea, some of the roughest waters in the world, in their winter. *Winnipeg* is accosted by four-metre waves, and she smashes through them majestically.

I'm on the bridge with JD, holding the tools for him while he fixes some bad wiring on one of the consoles. The motion is overwhelming. I watch while walls of water pass us and *Winnipeg* drops suddenly through a trough. Gravity disappears for a moment then returns double strength. There's a loud boom as her nose dips into the water, and the next wave rears up in front of us, smashing over the bridge windows.

"That's a good one," remarks the officer of the watch casually. The wiper blades work endlessly to clear the windows.

Most of the crew is affected by some amount of seasickness. The lines at the galley shrink during mealtimes, and I've lost my appetite. I snack on saltine crackers at a steady pace for the duration of the sail. Looking through endless mounds of technical manuals is low-grade torture during this motion. I spend my time bitter, dizzy, and alone. At night I strap myself into my rack with my seat belt and sleep badly.

I'm called to the coxn's office again. He explains I have a new punishment since I broke my signed agreement by having beer in the Cave. He tells me he rarely does this, but in my case he will instill the coxn's punishment rather than have me be charged again. He consults with the chief ERA, and they assign as punishment one of the dirtiest engineering jobs to be found. Once we come alongside in Melbourne I am to spend half the day scrubbing out grease from the steering gear machinery.

Carrying armfuls of rags, I head aft to the steering gear compartment now that we're alongside. I check to make sure that the steering gear pin is in place before I go to work; otherwise, if the rudder moves it will crush me like a bug. I spend the morning crawling into tight spaces wiping grease from all the moving parts. The chief ERA briefly inspects my work, reports to the coxn that I've fulfilled my punishment, then I'm walking away from the boat. I'm in Melbourne, Australia.

We're treated to a fleet of drivers sporting diplomatic plates and small Canadian flags on the hoods. They run a continual taxi service ferrying people from the boat to downtown. I wander around the arts district and strike up a conversation with a local who introduces himself as Mick. Before I know it, he's invited me back to his apartment and is cooking me dinner. He lives above the flower shop where he works. I have to return to the boat, but we make plans to meet up in the next few days.

There's a ceremony on the flight deck where we say goodbye to our old CO and XO. Commemorative plaques are handed out by chief heads of departments, and photos are taken. High-ranking people shake hands and smile perfectly. It's tradition for each Mess to give the departing CO a gift. He gets expensive bottles of scotch from the chiefs and POs. I clap with the crowd as Alders hands the CO the junior ranks' gift of a fishing rod. She looks perfect as she shakes his hand and smiles for the camera.

Back on the boat I get drunk. I walk into the Cave and start drinking vodka with orange juice. MS Hampton is there and he starts talking to me, all the while ordering me more drinks. This is the first conversation I've ever had with him. It turns out Hampton only talks to me when he's drunk. Normally he won't even look at me.

"You intimidate me 'cause you use such big words," he tells me through slurred speech. "You don't sound like a normal OD."

I don't know what to say to this so I take another sip of my drink. I lose track of how many drinks I've had and just keep drinking. I'm beyond caring. OS Linden comes to sit next to me and feeds me more vodka and orange juice.

"My life is in ruins." I'm slurring my words now as I turn to OS Linden.

I wake up in my rack lying in the recovery position. I'm briefly disoriented because the last thing I knew I was talking to OS Linden. I realize I must have passed out. It must have taken quite the effort to get me up to two deck and into my top rack. I don't have any new bruises. I feel endearment toward my shipmates. I trust them with my life.

I realize I have fifteen minutes before I start my upper deck sentry watch, and I jump down from my rack to dizziness, nausea, and a reeling feeling that tells me I'm still drunk. Oh shit.

I go to the Heads and brush my teeth twice. I hope I don't stink like booze. Someone is in the Heads vomiting, so I leave to use the other Heads farther aft before showing up at the fo'c'sle for sentry duty. I take the assault rifle from the previous sentry and put the bulletproof vest on. I'm handling a firearm while drunk. I spend the next four hours pacing around the upper decks trying not to throw up and hoping I don't have to shoot anyone. Some pleasure-cruising tourists get too close for comfort, within a few metres of the hull. It looks like they just want a good picture, but the Navy doesn't take any chances. I get to face them with my rifle obviously on display and gesture for them to back away.

Once my sentry watch is over I end up in a bar with most of the ship's company, and I'm drinking again. Suddenly the old EO comes up to me through the crowd and is gently pulling me by the hands onto the dance floor. He is quite drunk. He holds me close, and we dance to a slow song. He's leaving the ship in a few days' time. We have a new EO now.

"I've been thinking about things between you and Robertson," he tells me. "I've come to the conclusion that, ultimately, he had your best interests at heart."

The song is over, and he regards me at arm's length now. He searches my face to see if I agree with him. I'm gripped with a sudden confusion as my face smiles back at him. Maybe Robertson only had what my other superiors had told him about my behaviour. Maybe he *was* just trying to make me a more productive member of the shop.

"I wish you well," the EO says as he smiles and hugs me.

I'm sitting at another bar in Melbourne when a man with a Canadian accent comes to sit next to me. We start chatting, and I'm finding myself to be quite attracted to this person. He's covered in tattoos and has short, spiky hair. I start to tell him about how I'm here with the Canadian Navy, and he seems quite interested in hearing about it. I smile and flirt and finally he introduces himself as my new XO!

On my last night in Australia I hook up with Mick again. We go to a local bar and listen to live fiddle music, and he keeps his arm around me. We stay up all night and before I get in my cab he hands me a rose from his shop. I sneak the rose onto the ship and place it in my locker where it stays for the rest of the sail.

HOW TO USE A SOCKET SET

I sink into a timeless void again as we sail out of Australia. We have a new CO, XO, and EO. The plastic rabbit commemorating the old EO is taken down, and we don't know what to make of the new EO yet. I miss the old EO. When I'm not doing rounds or on watch or Turning-To, I'm either with Jed in the chart room or sleeping. More and more I just want sleep. My punishment duties continue to drag on; I continue to be shut away in the degaussing room organizing countless binders. On watch when all the lamp-ups are done, I stare bitterly at technical manuals while all around me people chat among themselves.

One day I'm helping Stafford with a lamp-up in the chief's and PO's Mess. I note the circuit number on the nameplate by the light, and we lock out the appropriate breaker. He stands close by chatting with one of the POs while I go to work disconnecting the ballast. I'm digging my screwdriver into it when a sudden jolt runs painfully up my arm. I yell, drop my screwdriver, and crumple inward cradling my arm. The POs are on me in an instant checking to make sure I'm okay.

Stafford gets angry at me for getting shocked and tells me, "You're working unsafely. This will be reported."

I'm confused because we locked out the breaker. It turns out the nameplate had a typo on it, and we locked out the wrong circuit. I try to share this important piece of safety info in the next shop meeting, but nobody cares. To this day that circuit probably still has the wrong nameplate on it.

PO 2 Perrant tells me to come with him one afternoon, and he leads me down to the forward AMR and finally starts to show me the generator. Except for draining the enclosure leaks, the generators have been giant grey boxes with unknown machinery until now. I'm thirsty for more knowledge now that all I do is stare at technical manuals and organize the library. Perrant shows me how to remove the enclosure doors, and I struggle to lift the sixty-pound door. The handle is well away from my centre of gravity. I have to fetch the aluminum extension handle, which lowers the door's centre of gravity, from the aft AMR.

Once the doors are removed, Perrant shows me a hatchway down in the bilge that he wants me to unbolt. I crawl down in the tight space between the generator and the catwalk. Perrant warns me to stay away from the shaft then. I glance over my shoulder, and the shaft is turning no more than a foot away from me. He hands me a socket set. I've never used one of these before, and he quickly shows me how it ratchets and how it fits onto the bolts. I go to work, reaching awkwardly with the tool into the generator. I loosen and remove the bolts. It feels good to be involved in fixing something, and to finally have my hands in her.

After my work is done, Alders pulls me aside and tells me coldly that it took me way too long to get that hatch off and that in the future if I wish to succeed as a marine electrician I need to work faster.

On another afternoon, Stafford takes me down to the aft AMR and waits impatiently while I fetch the aluminum extension handle to remove the enclosure doors. Once I have the appropriate door removed he shows me how to grease the bearings on DG3. DG3 thunders away noisily while I reach into hot, diesel-covered, blackened parts to attach the grease gun the way he shows me.

I'm walking down the flats one evening, and I'm just passing the shop when I overhear Stafford's voice mention my name. I pause at the door to listen in.

"She needs to use the aluminum extension to get the enclosure doors off. What if there's an emergency?" Stafford complains.

I remember the way Donalds threw off those doors during the fire.

"She'll make a terrible ETOW," Stafford snorts.

"Alders told me it took her way to long just to remove a hatch the other day," JD tells Stafford.

The next day I wake up to a tight pain in my neck. It hurts to turn my head. Perrant tells me to go to sick bay, so I do. The doc briefly inspects me while I stand there in my sports bra smelling his aftershave. He comes to the conclusion it's just a strained muscle and offers me some Tylenol.

I'm sitting in the Cave eating my dinner when all of a sudden MS Shelley is standing over me menacingly, her face just a few inches away from mine.

"OS Peffers, once again you forgot to clean the Mess," she tells me in a low, threatening tone of voice.

"I'm sorry, I'll do it as soon as I'm done eating." I sit feeling guilty, staring back at her. She stands there with her face in my face for a few more seconds, then she storms out of the Cave. Holloway, who is sitting across from me snorts and tells me she's a bitch.

Word comes down the chain that there's to be a ceremony on the flight deck one afternoon. I'm just getting off watch, and I'm looking forward to a nap. I ask MS Hampton when I should head out to the flight deck, and he tells me right at 1500. When 1500 rolls around the ship is suddenly deserted, and I walk through the empty flats and open the door leading to the flight deck. The entire ship's company has formed up early, and now they all get to see me stepping timidly onto the flight deck. I'm the last person to form up. People shake their heads and snort as I pass them to join my department in ranks.

We had a mail dump while in Australia. There is a pile of letters strewn about the counter in the Cave. While I eat I browse through them. It gives me something to gratefully focus on while no one talks to me. A huge pile of letters are from one woman who writes letters to soldiers all the time. She talks about her days and her garden and the weather. It's touching to hear these little stories, and it provides a distraction from the monotony. There's a pile of kids' pictures too. School kids have learned about HMCS *Winnipeg*, and they've sent pictures of swashbuckling cartoon, Disney-style pirates with parrots on their shoulders and hooks for hands. I'm told the majority of the letters and pictures stayed with the officers in the wardroom. It's not expected that junior NCMs would care about politics.

Drills still happen every afternoon, only now we have a new EO. Donalds also left the boat in Seychelles, and now my engineering officer of the watch is PO 2 Levette. Levette leaves me alone. I climb up to the chart room to hang out with Jed every day now. I bring tea, and we chat or complain to each other about being on ship.

"I forget after each deployment just how bad they are," Jed tells me, offering me the last of the chocolate-covered coffee beans.

"How was your mid-deployment leave?" I ask, trying to think of something positive to say.

"Wasn't long enough…or it was too long; it's weird. How was yours?"

"I broke up with my boyfriend," I say evenly.

"Oh, Peff, I'm sorry. How long were you together?"

"Five years…well, the last two were long-distance."

"I was on the commissioning crew for the *Ottawa* back in the nineties…it had the largest proportion of divorces from one sail… still keeps the record to this day."

"Really," I say, munching on the last few coffee beans.

"My first marriage was already over by then," Jed says thoughtfully.

"I see."

Jed sits in silence for a while, then turns to me, "Any more drama from Robertson?"

"Yeah, I'm getting feedback sessions as an additional remedial measure until the end of the sail," I snort.

"On top of the charges?" Jed sounds surprised. He whistles then. "Yeah, he totally boned you. Oh, Peff."

"I have to go, I'm on watch soon," I say. My voice sounds monotone. I jump down from the chart table and go to open the door. Suddenly Jed is up from his chair, giving me an awkward hug while I pull the door open. I return the hug briefly, feeling nothing, then I'm out into the flats again.

I have another feedback session in the aft switchboard. This time Robertson and Finley sit in front of me, and Alders stands in the background.

"OS Peffers, you may now talk about how the last few weeks have been for you," Robertson tells me after his speech.

Finley sits there so pleasantly. I know what they want to hear, and I give it to them.

"I've been learning from my mistakes and taking the time now to notice my feelings and taking a step back before I get angry," I say, making a good speech of it.

Finley nods approvingly.

"I've noticed you still have some difficulty integrating into the shop, but I do see an improvement in your conduct," Robertson tells me.

This is how it's going to be. I'm Robertson's project. It's complete bullshit; I'm just telling them what they want to hear. Robertson gets to look good now as he counsels the Insubordinate OD. No punishment ever reaches Stafford.

I'm putting my clean laundry away in my locker when I notice MS Shelley crying on the couch. She has always been mean to me. She's talking to Race Car.

"It's my partner back home..." Shelley sobs, "He's cheated on me."

"Oh, I'm so sorry to hear that," Race Car says in reply.

"I never thought..." Shelley sobs again, "I trusted him."

I stand there getting a sadistic pleasure out of hearing her woes. I slow down and spend as much time as possible putting my clothes away so I can maximize my time spent vindictively watching her cry.

GASH

I'm sitting in the aft switchboard again going through the ordeal of another feedback session with Robertson.

"OS Peffers, you'll be working in the dry gash compartment for the next seven days to help out the bosuns," he tells me.

Dry gash is one of the dirtiest jobs on ship and is a favourite for punishment duties. I sit there mute and angry with my face held as neutral as possible.

He goes on, "Once you're done in the dry gash compartment, you'll be molly again until we get home."

By the time we get back to Victoria I will have spent half the deployment as molly. Three full months. Still no extension on my training packages. Normally molly duty is supposed to last one month a year.

"Just a reminder about your previous attitude problems while working with PO 1 Davin," Robertson tells me evenly. "Once again I have to emphasize the importance of proper conduct."

As if I could forget. Finley sits next to him nodding and smiling sweetly.

It's my time to talk now, and Robertson wants to hear about how I've been doing over the past two weeks. I feed him more expected bullshit.

"I am confident I won't have any more problems with PO Davin now that I have my newly acquired emotional regulation skills," I tell him, keeping my voice as neutral as possible.

I finish by assuring him, "I will report to my shop master seaman at once if I feel frustrated in the future." Alders stands by the door staring at the deck.

Everyone seems quite satisfied as copies of paperwork are brought out, and I sign my signature again. I can't wait for these feedback sessions to be over.

I'm pulled off the watch rotation, and I no longer see the MCR or the machinery spaces. I report to the dry gash compartment and start working with OS Cornelle. Cornelle is being punished by her own department, and we spend a week working together as mutual outcasts.

All the ship's garbage that's not wet gash makes its way to the dry gash compartment. There, the glass and metal gets crushed and sent overboard, the cardboard and paper gets pulped and sent overboard, and the plastic gets melted down into thick plastic pucks which are stored in their greatly compacted form until we reach port and they can be disposed of on land. The Canadian Navy leads the world in environmental stewardship, not that that ever makes it to the news. I spend my days melting down mounds of plastic and shredding heaps of cardboard and paper.

Cornelle finishes cramming a few more plastic milk containers into her puck maker, expertly slams closed the lid because it's half-broken, then leans all her weight on the lid until the click is heard which means it's locking. The locking sensor is also half-broken.

She punches a few buttons then tells me very matter-of-factly, "I was charged in Basic Training. I was the shit pump of the platoon. I went AWOL. The instructors hated me and had picked on me endlessly."

She shifts her weight onto one foot and puts a hand on her hip thoughtfully. "I just couldn't get my shit together, I always had extra duties." Cornelle looks at me then and says, "People treat you like shit when you're in trouble here. But it gets better. Once people get to know you, they'll accept you more."

I'm busy in the adjacent puck maker, stuffing wads of old garbage bags and rancid food containers into the machine.

"Thank you," I say, smiling. It's one of the friendliest things anyone's said to me lately.

Cornelle goes on, "But in the meantime we're stuck in this shithole doing this disgusting shitwork." She kicks her machine affectionately. "So while we're here we'll be shit pumps together."

I laugh as we wrestle with my lid, which is even more broken than hers.

The work in dry gash is unsupervised so we take breaks whenever we want. As long as all the gash gets processed by the end of the day no one cares. I'm taking a break one afternoon standing aft of the port boat deck just outside the dry gash compartment. I'm trying my eyes at daylight for a change. It's overcast so it's not so bad.

Perrant walks up to me and stands next to me for a while. I'm expecting another lecture or more feedback, but instead he tries to talk to me. I think he feels guilty about what Robertson is doing. He's only a PO 2 though, so he can't go against the PO 1. I don't help him out with the conversation. I stand silently and watch him squirm as he tries to find things to ask me.

"How's it going, Peff?"

"Fine."

"Working okay with OS Cornelle?"

"Yup."

"Just another few days, then you'll be done."

I just stand in silence, looking out to sea. The silence stretches on and then I say, as an afterthought, "I suppose."

Perrant shifts his weight awkwardly and scratches his head. There's more silence, then he says, "You're doing a good job."

Then he turns and leaves, heading forward through the port boat deck to the CO's airlock to go down below again.

PADRE

In an example of true Navy planning, we get our padre after we leave the war zone. He joined the boat in Seychelles, and one afternoon when I'm almost done in dry gash he comes to find me to talk to me.

"You've been flagged because of all the trouble you've been in. Can we chat?"

We sit on the starboard boat deck, and I blink painfully in the bright sunlight. The starboard boat deck is where you go if you want to have a private conversation because it's almost always empty.

"So, how's it going?" he asks me in a friendly tone of voice.

"I'm fine," I shrug.

I'm not a religious person, but I appreciate the company. We chat for about an hour about all kinds of things, and he leaves satisfied that I'm doing okay.

Some people like a rebel, which is apparently what I'm being called now. At night, just after I finish as molly, I go to the port missile deck for a while, and this time LS Coté is suddenly standing next to me in the darkness. He starts to tell me about his rape fantasy where he gets to play the rapist. I'm suddenly very aware of how strong Coté is compared to me, how far away the port missile deck is from anywhere with people, how dark it is, and the droning machinery noise. I curse my size again and feel the familiar hunted and trapped fear.

We're coming up to our next port now, so people start pairing off.

"I'm looking for someone who's also into rape fantasies," Coté tells me.

"I have to go," I tell him. I walk briskly to the port bridge wing and then onto the bridge which is full of the dark shapes of people. I lean on my pole while my heart rate returns to normal. No one notices my presence.

I'm folding my clean laundry again and putting it away in my locker when I find out I'm missing half my underwear. I go back to the laundry flats and check the washer and dryer to make sure they weren't stuck to the inside of the barrel. I realize the only time anyone could just take them is when they're dirty and hanging in my laundry bag outside my locker. Otherwise they're locked inside my locker. I start to think about the implication then that someone has stolen my dirty underwear, and a shudder runs up my spine.

Now that we're out of the Box, bong-bongs have resumed at all hours of the day and night at random intervals. One afternoon the bong-bongs sound loudly throughout the ship. I drop the cloth that I had been using to wipe down tables in the Cave and automatically make my way to the forward section base. The pipe tells us there's a fire in the wardroom servery this time. I dress with the rest of the attack team, stepping into bunker gear that's way too big for me. I ignore this unsafe fact now. I hardly ever think about it anymore. The bunker gear is too big for me and probably always will be. It's always just a drill anyway, so getting a mask that fits...

"Let's go, people! This time it's real!" PO 2 Haro, the section base buffer, steps into the compartment with his headset and clipboard.

Adrenaline surges through me, and my heart skips a beat. I pause for a second and look at my mask in my hands. All around me people rush about, and no one cares that I'm going into a real fire with dangerously too-big gear. Suddenly I don't care either, and I swallow the nagging fear and finish getting dressed.

Thankfully the fire was able to be put out with fire extinguishers. I find out later that it was caused by a blown transformer. Thankfully I didn't have to fight a fire with a badly sealing mask.

We are sailing over the Great Barrier Reef, so we can't dump anything. The hull techs quickly construct a large bin aft of the port boat deck, and the mollies are instructed to put the wet gash in there. It's still hot outside, and the cooks take the time to clean out the freezers. By the time we're clear of the reef and we can resume dumping, mounds of old meat have been stewing in equatorial heat for days. I spend a few hours with the other mollies handling stinking rotting food with maggots crawling all over it. We wrinkle our noses, gag from the stench, and work as quickly as possible.

I'm in the chart room with Jed again.

"We're en route to Tonga now," he tells me.

"Oh, okay," I try to sound interested.

"The ship has bought an entire resort for an evening, and this is supposed to be our decompression port after our time in the Box," Jed tells me with a snort.

"Decompression port?" I ask.

"Yeah, we're supposed to be able to relax."

"You don't think that's possible in Tonga?"

Jed shrugs. "It's slightly possible, but Tonga isn't exactly a vacation spot."

We make plans to hang out again. By now it's thoroughly entrenched in common knowledge that the weather witch is fucking me. The woman is never presented as fucking the man; it's always the other way around. Every time Jed and I walk across the brow together, all the men stop and just stare at me.

"Guys come up to me and ask me how I managed to bag you," Jed tells me incredulously. We ignore the rumours.

One evening I decide to visit the bridge again. The officer of the watch welcomes me back and notes that he hasn't seen me in a while. I hug my pole in the darkness and watch all the various activities around me. Suddenly there's a voice whispering closely in my ear. I recognize the voice as Coté's.

"I can smell you," he whispers. I stiffen in the darkness, and a chill runs up my spine. No one else heard him. The fear hits me again, and I really hope he doesn't try to rape me. I stand frozen in place. Coté slips away into the darkness of the bridge.

TONGA

I wander around Tonga by myself for the first night while all around me groups of friends walk together. The next day we pile into buses that take us through lush banana trees and palm trees to a beach resort. I find Jed, and we sit together on the sandy beach with McNeil, the junior met tech. We start drinking early but soon discover that the rum here has been significantly watered down.

The food is cold hamburgers and bland mashed roots. In the afternoon we are given a traditional Tongan greeting ceremony involving drinking cava. It's a cloudy-looking bitter liquid that looks like dirt with water. There's a pig race where one of the little pigs breaks a leg and then in the evening there are performances from fire dancers, and a large pig is roasted and served to us. I am served a portion of the pig's fatty neck, and Jed gets a picture of me gagging while I try to eat it. We continue to drink into the evening, but we can't get very drunk with the watered-down booze.

On the last evening, Jed and I go out for Chinese food. It seems to be the only real restaurant on the island. The food is quite good, and this time the wine is full strength. We wander around Tonga at night and observe truckloads of young people driving about recklessly in the dark streets. There are very few street lights here. There's a kind of tension among the people, and Jed tells me about the monarchy in charge and how the Tongans aren't happy with them. There's very little effort in tourism here, and the Tongans would like to develop their tourism industry. Jed tells me Tonga is ripe for a revolution.

Back on the boat the rumour mill tells me that one of the junior officers overdosed on cava. He's being treated in sick bay and apparently ended up with tingling and numbness in his limbs.

I'm overwhelmed by new things. I return to the familiar routine of sailing as we slip and start to head home toward our last port which will be Hawaii.

INFAMOUS

The first morning we sail I head into the Cave to start my shift, and of course the Cave is a complete mess. MS Monro is sitting on one of the benches, hunched over and shaking. He looks terribly ill.

I go up to him and ask, "Do you need help getting to sick bay?"

"Fuck off," he mutters angrily.

I'm struck by his use of profanity toward me. Irritation stabs through me as I realize higher ranks can swear at me and get away with it.

Some bosuns come in for breakfast then and see him. They quickly hand him a beer, and I realize Monro is a complete alcoholic.

Now that I'm molly again, I'm forced to work with Davin. He generally ignores me or makes condescending remarks to me during the meetings, but I'm too numb to care anymore.

"Here's the schedule for the next leg of the journey," Davin holds a piece of paper in his hands as the mollies all surround him for the meeting. "No fucking around, especially you, Peffers, there's always work to do."

There's a pause while Davin stares at me, waiting. "What do you say, Ordinary Seaman?"

"Yes, PO," I say in a monotone.

Stafford is also molly now and has developed a chronically bad mood because of it. It's not long before he starts throwing hostile comments at me, and I reply with equally hostile remarks.

"You haven't changed the dishwasher water, Peff! I told you to do it twenty minutes ago!"

"I've been busy with the tables. In case you haven't noticed they were covered in grime!"

"I know it's hard for you, but work faster, damn it! Or no, let me guess, you forgot again!"

"I haven't forgotten, I can only do one thing at a time!"

"Bitch!"

"Asshole!"

Of course my behaviour gets reported to Robertson, and nothing happens to Stafford.

In the feedback sessions, Robertson is talking again: "You must treat your superiors with respect at all times," he reminds me.

I finally snap and tell him what I really think.

"My work environments are hostile and condescending, and my charges were a result of harassment. I think it's unfair that only I get punished!"

Finley's pretty face shows an innocent shock while I raise my voice in anger. All I get from it is Robertson reminding me, "OS Peffers, you need to control your temper and you can't speak to me in that tone of voice."

I also get a reprimand because I slipped into referring to Stafford as Tom (his first name) a few times during my rant. I indulge in some good old-fashioned eye rolling then and throw my hands up in frustration.

"You're behaving extremely inappropriately, and you're on the verge of getting charged again," Finley reminds me in her perfectly sweet voice.

Over the next few days I'm made to reread and sign to say I've read the Canadian Forces *Harassment Prevention and Resolution Guidelines*. Robertson approaches me for a signature to say that I've reread the guidelines. We're in the shop again.

"OS Peffers, would you like to conduct a third-party mediation between yourself and LS Stafford?" He has more paperwork in his hands.

I sigh apathetically, "Do you think it'll help?"

"It's designed to help resolve a conflict. It's shown to work in the past for similar situations; I think it's a good idea," he tells me.

"Okay, I agree. Let's try it."

"I'll approach LS Stafford and ask him the same question. Once you both agree we can begin," he explains.

Stafford doesn't agree to it, and so it goes nowhere.

I've become infamous. Rumours start to circulate about me doing all kinds of rebellious and insubordinate things that didn't even happen. Now in my feedback sessions Robertson starts by reviewing the rumours about me first, and I get to listen and shake my head and tell him those things didn't happen.

According to the rumours I'm seen quite often arguing with POs in the flats. I am single-handedly responsible for cancelling a racy sex-themed television show that was being shown in the Cave that I actually found to be hilarious, and I was seen fighting with various ODs at random times throughout the day.

I'm pissed off with the rumours, and now I have a pile of boxes to cut apart in the Cave before I carry the cardboard to the dry gash compartment. I take out my knife and stab savagely at the cardboard. Of course someone is sure to notice this, and the next day Robertson shuts me in the shop and I'm trapped again. My heart pounds as he tells me, "OS Peffers, you have been observed working unsafely with a knife while being molly."

There's a silence then and I simply stare at the deck. Anger is far away, through a wall of numbness.

"This is unacceptable behaviour, Ordinary Seaman," Robertson goes on. "It will be added to your file."

There's another pause while I feel my heart pound, and I continue to stare at the deck.

"This won't happen again, will it Ordinary Seaman?"

"No, PO."

"Good," Robertson opens the door and ushers me back into the flats.

There are a few dirty dishes in the scullery but not enough to run a load through the dishwasher. I sit down for a few minutes, and suddenly I'm reported as shirking my molly duties. I have to stand through a lecture from Davin: "There's plenty of work to do, and you can't just spend your time sitting around!"

He keeps ranting for a while but I tune it out. I stand there, eyes fixed on his eyes, noticing how small and piggish they are. I think about the pigs from Tonga, and my mind wanders to Chinese food with Jed. He's smiling and toasting me over red wine.

"Do you understand, Ordinary Seaman?"

I snap back to the present and say "Yes, PO," and I know those magical words will make him go away.

One morning Robertson tells me it's my turn to go up in the Sea King. Now that we're out of the Box the air det is flying the helo like an amusement park ride for the ship's company. I sit through the pre-flight brief where they review how to escape in the event the helo crashes into the ocean. I'm told it will flip upside down and fill quickly with water. I don a helmet and headset and strap in while we lift off from the flight deck. I watch as we move quickly away from *Winnipeg*, and suddenly she's so small and far away and all alone in a huge expanse of water.

The experience is wasted on me as I smile mechanically and observe numbly. I take pictures, and in the pictures it looks like I'm enjoying myself. I even get to sit in the pilot's seat and steer for a while. I tell myself to wake up, that I'm doing a once-in-a-lifetime thing right now—surely I should feel something. But I continue to experience things through an invisible wall that clearly separates me from the rest of the world.

One evening the PSP staff who joined us in Tonga give a presentation to us in the hangar. The helo is out on the flight deck to give us room. We crowd in and sit cross-legged on the deck. They reiterate things that I've never even heard of, like the deployment emotional cycle. I realize then that there's all kinds of pre-deployment info that I didn't have time to hear. They tell us about symptoms of PTSD and mention what's new in Victoria since we left. Victoria is still new to me so hearing about construction on various roads is lost on me. Everyone around me is looking forward to going home, and I'm looking forward to learning a new city. I hear sniffing through the crowd and look over to see Davin crying silently. I sit dry-eyed and numb. I think that if the wall were gone I would be feeling vindictive toward him. I will return single, and the person I love most in this world is a whole province away and always will be. There will be no one waiting for me on the jetty.

One morning I wake up to a different kind of motion. There's an unexpected wobble to *Winnipeg*, and I know something is wrong. I visit the MCR before I go to the Cave, and sure enough the on-watch stoker tells me they think we have a net wrapped around one of our props. The plan is to get the divers to go down and remove it once we're in Hawaii.

Alders takes me to my Div O's cabin again for another PDR. I sit on the couch and read. It states that I've been observed working unsafely on a number of occasions including not using safety glasses, inappropriate use of a knife, and purposely putting a known skin irritant (the blue silicon gel) on my skin and not removing it after I was ordered to. I continue to display inappropriate behaviour toward my superiors, and the example is when I rolled my eyes and raised my voice in one of the feedback sessions. I do not reflect favourably on the ship's company, and if I want to advance in my trade I will have to overcome these shortcomings.

I'm seething. I sign to say I've read and understood my PDR, and then I'm let out again into the flats.

It's night, and I go up to the flight deck. There's no moon, and it's pitch-black except for the millions of glittering stars above us. I lie down in the middle of the flight deck and stare up at the night sky. I'm completely drained. I feel the motion and watch the stars, and someone almost steps on me in the darkness. Suddenly they're asking me if I'm injured, and I hear my voice in the darkness. It sounds mechanical as I tell them I'm fine.

Jed has been listening to my frustrated stories, and now he invites me to do karate with him in the evenings. We stand side by side in the cramped dark-red hangar doing *katas*, and I find the repetitive motions to be soothing. I stand next to Jed, wearing a baggy t-shirt and shorts, in sync with his movements.

One evening, Jed brings out some sparring gear and shows me how to throw punches and kicks. He tells me to visualize Davin's or Robertson's face where I land my blows, and it's not long before I'm punching and kicking the anger out of myself with as much strength as I can muster. I almost knock Jed over and he tells me, "That was a good one!"

After only a few minutes of punching my knuckles are skinned raw, but Jed points out how most of the blood is on my first knuckle so my technique is sound. I ignore the pain and spend the next few weeks with scabs on my knuckles. Finley is horrified to see my skinned knuckles in my next feedback session.

Life drags on as if the sailing will never end. It seems the closer we get to home the slower time passes. Gradually the ocean temperature drops as we head back into the northern hemisphere. *Winnipeg*'s sea water circulation system grows colder again, but I'm not there to feel her pumps and motors anymore.

GATE SENTRY

We man the guardrails to show our respect as we come into Pearl Harbor and pass by the USS *Arizona*'s watery grave. We park at our jetty, and duty watches are assigned and the divers go to work cutting the net from our props. I forget to put a shake in to wake me up for my upper deck sentry duty and show up late. I'm told I'll be working a second duty watch as punishment. I don't really care.

Cpl Slater has been able to convince the famous comedian Russell Peters to come and give a show on the ship one evening. Russell Peters has heard about our adventures with pirates, and now he, uses us to spread more publicity about his work. The evening of the performance is the evening I do an extra punishment watch, and I'm stuck as a gate sentry down the jetty when the limo shows up with the comedian. I catch a brief glimpse of Peters leaving in the limo as he's driven away down the jetty, and I see a polite but inwardly disgusted smile. To a celebrity, we probably live like prison inmates. I wonder what he makes of our cramped home.

For our last evening in Hawaii I'm in a van with Jed, and we're heading into town. I'm sitting in the front passenger seat, and he's sitting directly behind me. Conversations swirl around me, and ever so gradually Jed leans forward and casually puts his hand on the back of my seat. His finger brushes lightly against my neck for the whole trip. Someone starts a discussion about who we'd fuck on the crew, and instantly Cornelle's name comes up as someone who's probably been banged by most of the crew by now.

"I'd never do that," Jed snorts. He's referring to Cornelle as an inanimate object. "Then there's you, Peff; you're like the wholesome girl next door."

I sit there silently, feeling another layer of loneliness wrap itself around me as my closest friend on the ship begins to sexualize me.

We slip for home, and Robertson leaves the ship in Hawaii to go home early for personal reasons. The rumour in the shop is that Robertson used to beat his wife, and now his kids hate him and he's an alcoholic.

My final feedback session is done by our new PO 1, PO 1 Kenneth. He sits alone with me in the aft switchboard. Kenneth is calm and soft-spoken, and he tells me, "According to the notes you've made a complete turnaround with regard to your attitude."

"That's good to hear, PO."

"Robertson thinks you are now officially well-integrated."

"That's good, PO."

Kenneth nods and continues, "I don't want you to be molly anymore; I think you've done enough of that for this trip. I'm putting you back on the watch rotation. You'll be working the same rotation as the rest of the ETOWs, one-in-three, six-hours-on-twelve-hours-off." He says it so kindly.

"Thank you, PO." I'm surprised. Maybe Robertson knew about the other ETOWs changing their watch rotation but just didn't do anything. I think I would be angry or frustrated to know that he kept me on one-in-four Turning-To so I got the least amount of sleep of all the people in the department, but the numbness is deep in my bones.

"You should have a clean slate now, Ordinary Seaman," Kenneth tells me brightly.

"That's good, PO." I manage to put some emotion into my voice.

A few months after we get back I put in a request for the boarding party course, and my new Div O denies it because of the charges and counselling from Robertson. According to him I still reflect poorly on the ship's company. So much for a clean slate.

I hoard sleep between my watches and begin to feel rested again. It's a strange feeling to not feel fatigue, and the past six months have passed in a hazy dream state.

My new-found rested state brings back the intense terror of the machinery spaces, and now when I do rounds by myself I try to approach the roaring, droning HP air compressor sitting angrily in its corner and I freeze, sweating, heart pounding. I force myself to continue to log it, stealing quick, hurried glances at its various dials, but something I just can't do now is check its sump. This requires you to stick your head less than a foot away from its thundering, rusted machinery parts because the sight glass is well out of the way in a corner. I stand there awash with shame because I don't want it to blow up while my head is right next to it. I suppose it would be a quick death, but I just can't convince myself to move any closer to it.

I put the logbook back in its cloth pouch and gratefully walk away from that beast of a machine thundering loudly behind me. I cringe as I dance quickly past the silent hydraulic start pack. It completely shames me that I can't seem to get over these fears. *Winnipeg* has been pushed hard over the past half year, and machinery is always breaking. It just seems like an inevitable matter of time before something violently explodes down here.

I'm in the dark-red hangar sparring with Jed again. He's laid a blue mat down on the deck, and he wants to show me some throws. He works me through the moves individually and when I'm ready he grabs me close and swiftly and firmly throws me onto the mat. I fall how he shows me, and we lie there. He continues to grip me for a moment too long, and I see his dark-red outline looming over me. We're very close, and suddenly I think it would be too easy to lift my chin up and kiss him. My heart aches with loneliness. I look away and start to scramble to my feet. He's married, I tell myself, although I get the impression that if I made a move he wouldn't stop me. The whole ship thinks we're fucking, but rumours are one thing and the real thing is another.

With less than a week to go people are climbing the bulkheads in a crazed desperation to be rid of this experience. I can almost taste my freedom. Tensions rise again as people cheer up as we get closer and closer. Jed's weather report jokes go from dirty to outright sick.

I'm in the chart room one evening, and all he can talk about is sex.

"I confess, Peff, through this whole damn trip you've made it bearable."

"Oh, thanks, Jed," I feel myself blush slightly.

"I have to admit, you've been my fantasy through it all."

I can't look at him. It seems everybody either hates me or wants to fuck me. I wonder briefly about whose rack my lost underwear is in. Feeling the familiar hunted, trapped feeling, I hear myself speak.

"Thank you," I say softly and slip out of the chart room.

THE BLACK DECK

I walk slowly through *Winnipeg*, drenched in the deep-red night lighting. I think about the nature of ships then and how they're referred to in the female. How they're used until they break. We crawl over her like ants. I trace my way through the flats, taking the time to notice every detail. I know all about her now, and everywhere I look I see a piece of machinery or pipe or cable and I know what it does. I don't really know where I'm going, and I keep walking. For once I don't need more sleep, and I still have a few hours before I have to start rounds again.

I wander down into the aft AMR and push through a wall of fear. I'm alone now in every way. I find the ladder then and I start to climb. Every step takes me farther away from the emergency escape hatches as I climb higher and higher. I freeze at the dirty black hatch, feeling trapped in terror. I can see a long way down below me to the hard, unforgiving thundering machinery.

I grip the wheel with my uniform sleeves wrapped around my hands and the heat spreads instantly to my fingers. I heave with all my strength and start to swear in frustration. I'm just a weak little girl, and nothing on this ship has been designed for me.

I'm sitting with my class at my trade training after Basic Training, everyone is uniform, sitting in neat rows. PO 1 Falmouth is writing on the whiteboard, and he pauses and turns to us briefly. He smiles over his shoulder in a knowing kind of way as he tells us, "Ships are female." I remember my initial reaction, the silent shock at his comment. I'm the only female in the entire class. But now I realize I'm just as sexist as him, the way I've been referring to her all along. I did it out of affection initially, then love. Does that still make it wrong?

Finally, sweating, I hear a pop and the wheel gives way. My grip slips on the hot metal then, and I almost fall. I cling to the ladder with a death grip. I'm a long way into *Winnipeg*, and no one knows I'm here. I don't want anyone to know I'm here. I push the hatch open and climb up into the hot, stinking Black Deck.

I close the hatch, and I'm drenched in utter blackness. I realize that the one remaining fluorescent light in this space has burned out since I was last here. I decide I'm not going to add it to the defect list because I simply don't care. I reach for my flashlight, and the little white light sends shadows dancing across black bulkheads and lights up the escape hatch in the deckhead in bright red. I sit down on the hard metal grating and lean against her dirty black insides.

What am I doing here? No one comes here unless they have to. I'm as deep inside her now as I can go, and farthest away from the endless stares of the men and the bitter glances of the women. I really wanted to be liked. More than anything.

It's a confused kind of relationship. I love my ship in a way I've never loved an inanimate object before, but every time I do rounds I'm terrified that she'll blow up. I feel the fear as I sit here in the hot darkness. I sigh heavily. Maybe it's just my own brokenness that I'm projecting. Maybe the cracks have already formed. Maybe it's me that's about to explode.

I'm walking into the recruiting centre in Edmonton for the first time. I'm shy but determined, taking in the green army fatigues for the first time. A lieutenant (Navy) welcomes me as I tell him I want to join the Navy. He ushers me into an interview room and starts to tell me all about it.

"The Navy is all about extending military power. Political influence. You don't win wars with a Navy, that's what the troops on the ground are for, but you definitely facilitate a victory." He pauses then continues: "The Canadian Navy is primarily peacekeeping oriented, even today with Afghanistan."

I nod my head, smiling excitedly. Peacekeeping sounds nice.

"When you sail, your ship becomes your home and the crew becomes your family."

I remember feeling something strong then, deep in my chest. It was longing. I wanted a new family ever since I left mine as soon as I could, at the age of eighteen. I realize now all I've done is traded one abusive situation for another.

I'm walking into the recruiting centre for the second time, a neat package of papers in hand that is my application to the military. I recognize the private who greets me as Meghan, someone I had gone to high school with in Fort McMurray. Now suddenly here we both are, smiling at each other. We go for a walk, and she tells me all about the travel and the pay and the job security that is unmatched by any other job. But mostly she tells me about belonging. I was sold. I was so tired of minimum-wage jobs or call centres. I was ready to invest in something, and I decided then and there that I was going to join the military.

Once Basic Training was over I was one of the up-and-coming young ordinary seamen. I was noticed by my instructors. I had the right attitude, the smarts, the right age, the right looks. The right gender. I approached all the right people and got posted to the *Winnipeg* after trade training because of the deployment. I wanted it, I went after it, and I got it. Out of all the people in my trade training class including the one with the highest marks, I was the only one who got their first choice of ships. I got the *Winnipeg* just as she was leaving, and I barely made the trip but the right people made sure I was there.

Now I have a long career ahead of me full of men who want to fuck me. I can never let my guard down. I can never feel safe. I realize now that I can never be one of the guys, and there are so few women in my department that we all stand alone. I've laid a trap for myself, and I've walked into it. It's snapped shut and I'm trapped. I don't know what to do.

CHANNEL FEVER

The night before we sail in to home port to the television crews and the cheering crowd, we hang back in the straits. It's always done like this. We arrive early and wait to make our grand entrance. That way we're never late. The final night before we go home is spent just off the coast of Victoria, and it's called Channel Fever. People pour onto the flight deck, and we do our best to polish off the last of the beer.

The rudder is set hard over, and we come to a full stop. We rotate in a slow circle then like a dog chasing its tail. The boarding party gets in the Zodiac and makes a trip to Tim Hortons and brings back coffee and donuts. We respond to a final distress call from a small fishing vessel that has run out of fuel, and we share some of our beer with them. I sit on the flight deck and drink down beer after beer. As usual no one talks to me. The conversations float around me and are full of excitement. Jed comes and finds me then and offers me a Corona from the chief's and PO's Mess. Coronas have special status on-board because they are only served to the senior NCOs. I take it like a peace offering, and we sit in a confused silence.

"I'm grateful for your friendship," Jed tells me then, and just like that the silence is easy again.

The following morning I get up and go through my washing routine one last time. The stares from the women around me seem less harsh, but I still haven't made any friends there. I skip breakfast since I'm hungover. We man the guardrails then, and I fall in at attention on the fo'c'sle. The helo takes flight, and one of the pilots hangs from a harness and bungee cord waving a large Jolly Roger flag that was made for the ship but since it wasn't an official maritime flag we couldn't fly it. We make five knots proudly flying our war banner, a large Canadian flag that looks to be a storey high.

The band strikes up and the music floats over to me as we approach a large crowd of cheering strangers, other people's families with Welcome Home banners. The cameras are rolling, and the helo flies behind us and we come alongside then. Heaving lines are thrown, engines are stopped, and the brow is lifted into place. I have thirty days of post-deployment leave looming in front of me, and then Robertson will be our PO 1 again. But for now it's officially over and behind me. Right now *Winnipeg*, with all her overworked, breaking, rusted charm, is home. Fresh water pump #2 is still running hot.

LIFE AFTER DEPLOYMENT

The deployment wasn't real. It occurred in some alternate reality. What's supposedly real is the life I have now, but I'm frozen. Time doesn't pass normally. Years go by, yet it feels like I just got back.

As soon as we got home, the ship's company was broken up, never to be together again. Within thirty days of returning, people were posted to different ships. People went on training courses. People who were brought on-board from other ships were sent back to their original postings. I miss my shop like I miss a bunch of old friends, even Stafford. They're still so clear in my mind just like I saw them yesterday. I don't understand this attachment, even though I feel it.

I got thirty days of leave once the ship returned home. I spent the thirty days drinking alone in my barracks room, watching the entire series of M*A*S*H. A few days after my leave was over, I showed up for work on ship one morning to a pipe from the XO.

"Good afternoon, *Winnipeg.*" The XO sounds very sad. "I just want you to put down whatever you're doing right now and listen."

I'm in the cleaning gear closet with OS Marriot when we both stop to listen.

"Someone's died," I say ominously.

"OS Cornelle was found this morning dead in her apartment..."

OS Marriot gasps. My hand flies to my mouth. We both look away from each other. I remember Cornelle then, smiling at me from her puck maker in the dry gash compartment. She had told me things would get better. Oh, how I wish I could have told her that yesterday. I instinctively knew it was a suicide, even though it was only later on that I got proof. The last time I saw her alive, she was a brow sentry, leaning on her podium on the flight deck, dark shades covering her eyes completely. She appeared to be staring off into space.

OS Chelsea, one of Cornelle's best friends, tells me of the suicide note she heard about from Cornelle's mother. The rumours of the harassment Cornelle experienced couldn't be proven since a lot of her div notes went missing. An anonymous Military Police tip informed me that she was also sexually assaulted.

Almost immediately upon returning to work on *Winnipeg*, I'm charged again by Robertson. He traps me alone in the shop for a little meeting. "OS Peffers, you were late crossing the brow this morning, as observed by the brow sentry."

"Yes, PO."

"What time does leave expire at?"

"0750, PO."

"The brow sentry logged you in at 0800. Late."

"Yes, PO."

"Why were you late?"

"I slept through my alarm, PO."

"And why did you sleep through your alarm?"

Because I drank too much last night and was still passed out, I thought to myself. "I don't know, PO, I just… didn't wake up when my alarm went off."

Robertson sniffs, "You are often late for shop meetings in the morning."

"Yes, PO." Inwardly I disagree with this, since leave expires at 0750. He wants me in the shop before 0750. Others, like Alders, can wander in at 0751, and he doesn't complain about it.

"I'm going to recommend charges be laid. You need to learn to be more punctual. You may go now." Robertson opens the door, and I gratefully walk out into the freedom of the flats.

There was another trial. I was charged the minimum amount again: seven days of punishment duties and a $150 fine.

I'm drinking every day when I hear about Alders' drinking binges from Alders herself. It's 1000, time for soup, and the entire ship's company stops working for twenty minutes to down a bowl of soup in the Cave. Alders sits across from me at our table.

"I drink so much sometimes, I wake up just covered in puke, amazed I'm still alive!" She laughs then before taking a sip of her soup.

We get a new OD, OS Reynolds, who is quickly given more responsibility than me.

The last thing I needed to get signed off on my package to get my watch was to run a blackout drill. This is when the ship loses all power, and the ETOW needs to restore full power to the entire ship.

I sat at my console in the MCR waiting for the blackout. Suddenly we're plunged into almost darkness as the emergency lighting comes on and a myriad of alarms come in from all the consoles, screaming for attention. My heart starts pounding.

My fingers fly over my console, pressing the various buttons to put a generator on load. I try a few times, but the generators won't be put on load automatically. I'd have to do it from the switchboards manually. It means something else has broken in the switchboards.

"I can't get a generator to go automatically, I'll have to do it from the switchboard!" I say over the din of alarms. I grab my ET tool bag and head aft at a quick walk to the aft switchboard. Robertson follows me like a shadow with a clipboard and pencil in hand.

I press a few buttons on the switchboard, but again the generators refuse to be put on load.

"You have permission to do it completely manually," Robertson says from beside me while he takes notes.

"But that removes all the safeties," I say with trepidation. I get the fear again.

"It's all part of your training, Ordinary Seaman!" he replies.

"I've never put a generator on load completely manually before, I don't know what to do."

Robertson points to a panel at the bottom of the switchboard and tells me to remove it. I do and see a few buttons. He points with his pencil at the button to press. But there's something wrong. My feelings of trepidation mount. There are already some lights back on in this compartment, which means we already have a generator on load, I just don't know which one. The indicating lights on the board are burnt-out so I can't tell.

"There's something wrong, PO."

"Just press the button, Ordinary Seaman."

"I've never done this before. It states quite clearly in my training package that I'd be shown all my work before I'm expected to carry it out."

Robertson sighs deeply in exasperation and leans in, pressing the button to put the generator on load with no safeties.

BOOM! There's a sudden loud noise, and we're both thrown backwards by a magnetic field. Smoke is now curling its way up and out of the switchboard.

"Do we have a fire?" I say, starting to look forward to just dealing with a fire as opposed to a blackout drill.

Robertson sighs again, picking himself up from the floor. "No, stay here." Then he's gone from the room.

Robertson had gone to the MCR to end the drill and to inform everyone that we'd just blown a breaker.

Later on that day, the burnt-out breaker is removed from the switchboard and brought into the MCR for inspection. PO 2 Perrant lets me examine the breaker. It's large and heavy. He points with his finger at a blackened part inside.

"That's the arcing chamber. It's designed to catch the flash and the arc so you aren't blinded or badly burned."

"Wow," I say, fingering the burnt piece. I'd been waiting for something like this to happen. For something to blow up. And now it has.

"PO 1 Robertson should have noticed that we already had a generator on load. What happened when he pressed the button manually was that a second generator tried to go on load out of sync with the first one. You're lucky no one was hurt."

I get my watch conditionally even though the new EO tells me I did the best he'd ever seen at my oral board. It's Robertson's idea to give me a conditional watch.

More time goes by, and I continue to drink every day. If I stop drinking a terrible anxiety grips me and I can't sleep.

We're all brought together again for the last time in 2010 in the ceremony where we are presented with our medals. The admiral leans into me as he shakes my hand and tells me: "Nice to have some colour on you so soon, eh?"

I respond with the appropriate "Yes, sir," but by then I know my career is over. I'll never have an opportunity to wear my medal. My picture appears in Victoria's *Times Colonist* newspaper shaking the admiral's hand.

Just before I leave *Winnipeg*, the entire Navy marches in dress uniform through downtown Victoria in the 2010 Freedom of the City parade. Alders is late for forming up for the march but isn't charged.

It's normal to give six months for people to find lodgings outside the base after their classes are completed, but Robertson forces me out of barracks early. I find an apartment in town, and my possessions are brought out of storage again.

I start smoking marijuana every day. It's better than alcohol for the anxiety because there's no hangover. I spend my free time curled up stoned on my couch. I'm not really living anymore.

I'm compassionately posted off *Winnipeg* to get me away from Robertson. This is how the Canadian Forces really handles harassment. The victim is removed. Not the perpetrator. The perpetrator is almost always higher in rank and is therefore needed operationally so the ship can sail. Ordinary seamen are always expendable.

"I'm compassionately posting you off the ship," Dr. Lenze, my psychiatrist at the base hospital tells me. He fills in some paperwork at his desk while I watch.

"Where will I be posted to?"

"There's room at the Naval Tender Section or NTS for a marine electrician; I'm sending you there instead. That way there's no sailing. You can focus on getting better."

"But I need to sail to keep up my experience with the ships so I can do my job."

"You need to focus on yourself right now, on getting better."

I sit in silence while he finishes the appropriate paperwork. I feel saddened at leaving *Winnipeg*, relief that I won't be around the machinery spaces anymore, and frustrated that my training is now over.

NTS is a unit that handles all the Orca sail training vessels for officer navigation training. At first I'm attach posted which means my official unit is still *Winnipeg*, but I show up for daily work at NTS. I now have a new PO 1.

I sit down one day at home in my apartment while stoned. I'm seized with a sudden urge to write. I find paper and a pen, and the words flow out of me. The groping, the pick-ups from the men. I hand my writing to my new PO 1 the next day at work. This was someone I could trust, a nice, competent professional PO 1. My new safe posting to NTS. Now that I'm safe I can start to talk. Or rather, start to write. I hand him the writing but can't say a word. He reads the first few sentences and assures me he'll pass it right up to the chief.

The chief of NTS is crusty and Old School Navy. He sits me down for a chat and tells me that men are pigs. This is a nice way of saying "buck up" to me about my complaint. He passes me down to the master seaman, and she helps me write and expand on what are now being called "allegations."

WORTHLESS

I start to get suicidal thoughts, and I go to the trusted new PO 1 like a well-trained soldier and ask for help. I manage to blurt out that the only reason I'm still alive is because I smoke weed every day; then I go mute. He sits with me for what ends up being hours trying to get me to talk. The only way I can communicate is to shake my head.

Officially, the CF has a comprehensive treatment package for addictions issues. Personnel are sent to Edgewood, a recovery centre close to Victoria. My doctor decided that I wouldn't be sent there since he thought it would just trigger me being around a bunch of alcoholic Navy guys.

I go home. I don't really want to live anymore. I take an over-dose of the medications I'm now on for apparent bipolar disorder. The large dose of antipsychotics makes my heart go into a scary, fluttering fast pulse that gives me chest pains. I panic. I don't want to die from a painful, lonely heart attack; I just want to fall asleep and not wake up. I thought I had complete control over my own death, but suddenly I am helpless. I call an ambulance. With my last strength, I crawl to the door, unlock it like the operator tells me, then pass out on the floor. Then I'm vividly standing in the smoking area at NTS with people all around me. It's clearer than a dream. MS Scott throws her cigarette butt onto the ground, grinds it under her boot and says, "That's it. I'm out." Walks away. I suddenly know if everyone around me leaves, I'll die.

The paramedics wake me by painfully pinching on my trapezius muscles. Force me to walk to the ambulance. Force me to sit, not lie down. They keep me talking.

"So you were on the *Winnipeg*?" My head turns automatically and through a thick haze I hear my slurred reply: "You know her name."

At the hospital's emergency room there's a police officer standing next to my bed. I pass out again. A doctor wakes me by pinching the back of my neck. I'm lucid long enough to answer his simple questions which I can't even remember now. I wake up hours later, and the nurse tells me I was in a light coma. The police officer is still there with her holstered gun.

News of my attempted suicide goes to the *Winnipeg*, since I'm still attach posted to NTS at first. Before I know it I'm being interviewed by a major. He looks me straight in the eyes and asks, "Is it fair to say that Robertson made you feel worthless?"

Worthless. It was the perfect word that I couldn't find on my own. I was perfectly worthless. Not felt, but was perfectly worthless.

Nothing more comes from the interview with the major.

Sometimes I tell myself I was just trying to get some sleep and just took too much medication by accident. I get confused. Motives are weird especially when you are worthless. Things lose their meaning. Maybe it doesn't matter what I was intending to do. I feel shame because of it. Think I'm a coward.

When I start seeing a psych nurse for art therapy at the base hospital, half of the things I create, a few paintings and a sculpture, go missing. I still want them back. I'm facing a medical release that I don't want. I still don't, and I'm out now. I just want to go back to *Winnipeg*. I think I will want this for a long time, maybe even the rest of my life. I'm told it's the PTSD. I had to push for that diagnosis though. The bipolar label was so automatic.

One day at NTS, the entire section is scheduled to go to the shooting range to do some target practice. I'm feeling too anxious to be handling a firearm so instead I go to the base hospital. The med tech who looks me over and gives me some Ativan talks while he fills in some paperwork at his desk.

"You know," he says, leaning back in his chair. "If you go to Afghanistan and come back with issues, you have PTSD. If you go anywhere else in the world and come back with issues, you have bipolar disorder. Just a trend I've noticed."

FLASHBACKS

My first flashback happened while I was boiling water in my kettle. I was impatient and absently felt it with the back of my hand to see if it was hot enough yet. And WHAM I'm back on *Winnipeg* feeling the motors again. Fresh water pump #2 to be exact. Before it ran hot. It was the same temperature as the kettle. This time I'm not numb. I'm filled with fear and a terrible isolation that goes beyond lonely, and I crumple into a fetal position on my kitchen floor. For the next two days I'm too anxious to leave my apartment.

My second flashback happened when I was at a party. Someone handed me a beer. When I opened the can I tasted the deployment. It was the exact same beer that I drank in the Mess: Kokanee. WHAM. I'm sitting in a crowded Mess completely alone, no one notices me. But this time I'm actually feeling the aloneness that spirals into extreme panic, and I curl up in a ball laughing hysterically. Uncontrollably. Why laughing? I have no idea.

My third flashback happened while I was on a medical training course. We were doing a test scenario using fake nautical-themed medical emergencies. The instructor's tone of voice goes very serious as he gets into character and does too good an acting job. He tells us we just got another distress call and WHAM. I'm back in the Gulf of Aden with the pirates only this time I feel terror. Suddenly out of control, confused, gasping, I repeatedly shout "No! No! No!" Dizzy, I sit down with my head in my hands.

I CAN NEVER GO BACK

The medical release marches on indifferent to what I want. It's been decided that members who are diagnosed as bipolar are to be medically released, no exceptions, no choice. I just want to go back to my ship. But I can never go back. I'm posted to IPSC which is where all the sick, lame, and lazy eventually end up on their way out. It is here that I compose my official written complaint document that's sent to Ottawa and comes back almost a year later; every single allegation is shot down due to for-matting errors or lack of witnesses.

Next, I apply for disability benefits with VAC (Veterans Affairs Canada) for PTSD. It's denied. The justification? It was not caused by military service as none of the allegations could be proven. I apply for disability benefits with VAC for bipolar disorder. It's denied. According to VAC, bipolar disorder is genetic and not environmentally caused. There's no history of bipolar disorder in my family. During my treatment, lithium didn't work either.

I approach the Military Police for the groping incidents, but they close the case without even an investigation.

Two MPs meet me in the lobby of my building and pull out their notepads.

"Good day, Ms. Peffers," one of them says to me.

"Good day," I reply, my heart pounding with nervous energy.

"So we've gone over the tape from your interview, and we've come to a decision not to investigate," the other one says to me.

"Why is that?" I feel nothing all of a sudden, except my heart hammer-ing in my chest.

"Your allegations," starts the first one, "don't meet the definition of assault under the Criminal Code of Canada."

I look at the floor for a second while this sinks in.

"So what is the definition of assault under the Criminal Code of Canada?" My voice sounds indignant.

"That's not for us to define, we're simply passing along information today," the second one tells me.

I relayed this information to my lawyer, Mr. Gordon, over the phone.

"That's ridiculous," he tells me. "Any unwanted sexual touching anywhere on the body is the current definition of sexual assault under the Criminal Code of Canada."

"What are my options?"

He sighs deeply over the phone. "There's not much more I can do. You are bound by the military legal system. I'm sorry."

Pages from my copy of my police statement go missing, and I pursue a complaint against this with the Military Police Complaints Commission. It is decided that there was no evidence of a conduct deficiency in the investigation. A second investigation was launched regarding sexual assault, and the Military Police claim they couldn't establish a clear motive for the perpetrators so the investigation is closed with no charges being laid. One thing came out of that investigation that was a breakthrough: the Military Police were told by the complaints commission to take allegations of sexual assault more seriously in the future.

Even after getting a psychologist's letter stating my PTSD was attributable to service, VAC still denies my claim based on lack of witnesses.

In an effort to get witnesses, any witnesses at all, I approach Jed who was posted to Ottawa soon after we got back. He stops talking to me instantly. We had been corresponding over email. Now there's only silence. Our friendship is probably over. Jed was the only one who witnessed me talking about the harassment and assault while in the chart room. He would have counted as a witness.

Six months before my release date in 2012, I'm allowed to start my re-education process. To rehabilitate me, I get two years of schooling paid for. I try to go back to university to finish my degree but sink into a horrible depression and withdraw from all my classes. Then I decide to go off the medications because the side effects cause me so much fatigue.

FUGUE

I start having amnesia and wake up not knowing how I got to be lying down on the road just outside the gate to the base. I'm confused and scared as police are patting me down. I don't want them to touch me. (Just don't touch me!) I keep flinching, and they keep having to start over. I remember sobbing while I beg them to stop touching me.

Another time I suddenly wake up inside an ambulance, and the paramedic is pinching me painfully on the wrist with my watch strap. I have no idea to this day how I got there or what I did to get picked up by the paramedics. They were very nice to me and dropped me off in the hospital parking lot and told me I was free to go.

I'm out of the military for five months when I end up in jail for assaulting a police officer. I have no memory of this. Apparently I was found walking among traffic with no concern for my welfare. They realize I'm mentally ill, and I'm sent to a forensic psychiatric hospital where I'm shut away in solitary confinement for two stints of five days each. I spend a total of thirty days in that psychiatric hospital.

I remember I was enraged while shut away in my cell; I kept kicking the door over and over again. The person in the cell next to me starts kicking his door and he's yelling at me to stop making so much noise. The guard tells him to settle down or he'll be up on more charges. I realize that they are letting me kick and yell all I want, but I don't know why.

Everything adds up. I realize I need the medications after all. My new civilian psychiatrist, Dr. Mason, tells me on our first visit, "They had you on a lot of medication for someone of your size." He writes me a new precription and I go back on the meds. This time the side effects are not so bad, and I'm less fatigued.

I decide to go back to school. I return to what is familiar and apply to train as a civilian electrician.

HOW I REMEMBER HER

I see parts of her everywhere. The antennae and satellite dishes on roofs of buildings. The fire mains painted red running through basements. Fire extinguishers, fire hoses, and compressed-air bottles. Yellow cargo straps. Diesel fumes mixed with the smell of deep-frying. The little motors and switches and multimeters that make up my life as a civilian electrical apprentice. And the fear is still with me. It's in the transformer that blew when my mask didn't fit in the real fire. It's in flipping large industrial breakers after one blew up in my face. Even car batteries scare me.

In a lab at electrician school we're working on capacitors, which hold power and release it suddenly when desired. I didn't even want to touch the capacitors, but I forced myself to, heart pounding, sweating at my workbench. We had to demonstrate touching the capacitor with a conducting piece of wire to show the quick arc that demonstrates the discharge of electricity from the capacitor. I just couldn't bring myself to touch the wire to the capacitor. I was convinced the capacitor was going to explode. Everything related to electricity just scared me. Working as an electrician didn't pan out for me. I was far too jittery.

FINDING A PLACE

I wanted a complete change but the Registered Massage Therapist and the Acupuncture program were too expensive. I chose Practical Nursing and put my name on the two-year wait list. While waiting for the nursing program to start, I got a job at a local bookstore and lived in constant fear of getting in trouble. I was never in trouble with management ever, but I just couldn't shake the foreboding that my reprimand or termination was just around the corner. Every single time my name was announced over the PA system to call management I just knew I was in trouble again. My heart would pound and I'd begin sweating. But it was always just to convey a shift change or something mundane. One night, the manager asked me to stay behind to help set out some book displays. I thought, this is it, this is how you fire someone, get them alone at the end of their shift. I went about my shift thinking it would be my last. It turned out the manager legitimately just needed some help with a book display.

The bookstore liked my performance so much that when I quit to go back to school, they said I would always be welcomed back.

Finally my name came up for the Nursing Program. After passing the prerequisite courses I enthusiastically jumped into my new life as a caregiver in the fall of 2016. The program was very intense, twelve-hour days plus weekends, and after a month I was exhausted and I had fallen behind. My psychologist took one look at me and told me she would get me a compassionate withdrawal. Veteran's Affairs pulled me from the Vocational Rehabilitation Program, so I can no longer work or go to school. I was told I can apply for the program again once I'm well enough to succeed at school.

Anxious thoughts are a part of my daily life now, even with medications. I take pills for my anxiety, depression, psychosis, and so I can sleep. I have been told that this "hyperarousal" is a common symptom of PTSD.

Slowly things resolve themselves, and I calm down. Then one day I wake up and realize I'm content. I begin to put a concerted effort into finding new friends. I start writing and I begin to meditate at my local Shambhala centre and explore Buddhism. Everyone at the centre is very polite and welcoming, and I begin to attend weekly meditations.

The medication and fear is just a part of my daily routine now. But the fear reminds me that I'm alive, and that this new life that I've built is mine alone. I no longer see myself as worthless.

GLOSSARY OF NAVY SPEAK

AC plant: air conditioning plant

AER: aft engine room

air det: air detachment

air detachment: the helicopter and its crew

AMR: auxiliary machinery room

baby doc: junior physician's assistant

banyan: a BBQ held on the flight deck once a week

BIRDS: Boys In Real Deep Shit

black water: sewage

bong-bong: call to action stations or emergency stations

bosun: boatswain

Box: a war zone where a ship is deployed

bunker gear: firefighting gear

Cave: Slang term for junior ranks Mess, where the junior ranks take their meals and socialize

CBRN: Chemical Biological Radiological Nuclear

Cdr: commander (Naval rank)

CF: Canadian Forces

closed up: describing a boat when everyone is at their station

CO: commanding officer

combat camera: military photographer / imagery technician

coxn: coxswain

coxswain: the highest-ranking senior NCO, in charge of the ship's discipline

CPF: Canadian Patrol Frigate

Cpl: corporal (Army rank)

CPO: chief petty officer

DC: damage control

design waterline: the area around the hull of a ship that designates what part of the hull is above and below the water line

DG: diesel generator

Div O: divisional officer

double-bank: to put a person in training on watch with someone already trained who has their watch ticket; the trainee is referred to as double-banked

duff: baked goods

DWL: design waterline

EO: engineering officer

ERA: engine room artificer—highest ranking stoker on-board, the chief head of department for the engineering division

ET: electrical technician

ETOW: electrician of the watch

FER: forward engine room

fo'c'sle: short for forecastle

gash: garbage

grey water: waste water from the sinks and showers

GT: gas turbine

hard sea trade: any trade in the Canadian Forces where the majority of your work is carried out on ship; some navy trades have the majority of the work carried out on land instead; those would not be hard sea trades

Heads: washrooms

hull tech: a hard sea trade dealing with all the structural functions of the ship such as door and hatch maintenance

in routine: whenever a CF member is posted to a new base or ship they must hand-carry a file folder around that base or ship and get a list of items signed off at various areas to show they have arrived, for example post office, stores, etc.

IPSC: integrated personnel support centre

lamp-up: to change a light bulb in the navy; the term originated back when oil lamps were used

LRAD: Long-range accoustic device

LS: leading seaman

Lt(N): lieutenant (Naval rank)

machinery control room: the compartment with all the computer monitors and controls for propulsion, power generation and damage control measures

MCR: machinery control room

Mess: any area on the ship designated for eating, socializing or sleeping

met tech: meteorologist

molly: dishwasher

MS: master seaman

nav comm: naval communicator—trade responsible for all forms of communication ship to ship

navy shower: a shower involving minimal water

NCM: non-commissioned member

NCO: non-commissioned officer (ranking below officers, middle management)

NTS: Naval Tender Section

OD: ordinary deckhand, slang term (pronounced "ode")

on watch: to be working in the watch rotation; a person is off watch when they are considered not currently working and having free time

OOW: officer of the watch

ordinary deckhand: equivalent to ordinary seaman in an older ranking system

OS: ordinary seaman—lowest rank in the navy equivalent to Army private

padre: chaplain

PDE: propulsion diesel engine

PDR: personnel development report

pipe secure: to signal the end of the work day

PO: petty officer; First Class outranks Second Class

PSP: civilians in charge of physical fitness who accompany deployed members

PUP: Personnel Under Punishment

RAS: refuelling at sea (pronounced "raz")

scooby bucks: local currency

SCOPA: senior commanding officer presently afloat

shincom: shipboard internal communicator

slip: leave the jetty

souvies: souvenirs

stoker: marine engineering mechanic

stores: the place where personal equipment is stored and handed out as needed

Turning-To: a regular 8 a.m. to 4 p.m. workday

uninterruptible power supply: battery power for essential systems in the event of a blackout when the ship loses all electrical power

upper deck: see weather deck

UPS: uninterruptible power supply

VAC: Veteran's Affairs Canada

watches (the twenty-four-hour period is broken up into four-hour watches):

> Mids: 0000 to 0400 (12 a.m. to 4 a.m.)
>
> Morning: 0400 to 0800 (4 a.m. to 8 a.m.)
>
> Forenoon: 0800 to 1200 (8 a.m. to 12 p.m.)
>
> Afternoon: 1200 to 1600 (12 p.m. to 4 p.m.)
>
> First Dogs: 1600 to 1800 (4 p.m. to 6 p.m.)
>
> Second Dogs: 1800 to 2000 (6 p.m. to 8 p.m.)
>
> Firsts: 2000 to 0000 (8 p.m. to 12 a.m.)

weather deck: any area on the outside of the boat

weather witch: meteorologist

WO: warrant officer, an NCO Army rank

workup: a short sail where the crew is tested through war games and DC scenarios

XO: executive officer

ACKNOWLEDGEMENTS

I would like to thank both my editors: Betsy Warland for her precious and patient tutoring, and Betsy Nuse for her editing skills. And none of this could have been possible without the financial support of my father, Chris Peffers.